THE ESSENTIAL CAMPING COOKBOOK

scouts
be prepared . . .

THE ESSENTIAL CAMPING COOKBOOK

OR HOW TO COOK AN EGG IN AN ORANGE

AND OTHER SCOUT RECIPES

**FOREWORD BY BEAR GRYLLS,
UK CHIEF SCOUT**

NICK ALLEN

First published in Great Britain in 2012
by Simon & Schuster UK Ltd
A CBS Company

1 3 5 7 9 10 8 6 4 2

Simon & Schuster Illustrated Books
Simon & Schuster UK Ltd
222 Gray's Inn Road
London
WC1X 8HB

www.simonandschuster.co.uk

Simon & Schuster Australia, Sydney

Simon & Schuster India, New Delhi

A CIP catalogue for this book is available
from the British Library

ISBN 978-1-47110-054-3

www.scouts.org.uk

The Scout Association Registered Charity no.
306101 (England and Wales) and SC038437
(Scotland) Incorporated by Royal Charter.

Editorial Director: Francine Lawrence
Senior Commissioning Editor: Nicky Hill
Project Editor: Abi Waters
Designer: Miranda Harvey
Home Economist: Richard Harris
Stylist: Tony Hutchinson
Commercial Director: Ami Richards
Production Manager: Katherine Thornton
Photography: Richard Faulks except:
p.6: Allan Baxter/The Scout Association and p.7:
Martyn Milner/The Scout Association
Photographer's Assistant: Oskar Proctor

Colour reproduction by
Dot Gradations Ltd, UK
Printed and bound in the UK by
Butler Tanner & Dennis Ltd

Notes on the recipes

All of the recipes in this book provide the standard
metric and imperial measurements, but they also
include a standard camp mug measurement so that you
can easily measure your ingredients without having to
take scales with you. As a guide, 250 ml
(8 fl oz) liquid = 1 normal camp mug.

Use one set of measurements only and not a mixture
of both.

All cooking methods are a guide only – please
feel free to change the cooking method to suit
your campsite, but do be aware that cooking times may
be affected.

Spoon measures are level.
1 tablespoon = 15 ml,
1 teaspoon = 5 ml.

Medium free-range eggs have been used unless
otherwise stated.

This book contains recipes made with nuts. Those with
known allergic reactions to nuts and nut derivatives,
pregnant and breast-feeding women and very young
children should avoid these dishes.

CONTENTS

FOOD ALWAYS TASTES BETTER OUTDOORS . . .

I've eaten some pretty unusual things in my time, and not always pleasant! You'll be pleased to know that this book will not be teaching you how to cook a sheep's eyeball or a hairy tarantula!

This isn't survival, instead it is the outdoors made tasty and amazing. It is about delicious selections of outdoor dishes that anyone can create. This means everything from fresh trout cooked in newspaper in the embers of your fire, to creamy mushroom risotto and old favourites like the damper.

What I love about this book is not just the recipes. It's packed full of advice on the techniques scouts have used for decades to make great food in the great outdoors. From how to make your own oven, to burying your porridge before you go to sleep so it's still hot in the morning, you'll discover tricks and tips that will amaze your friends and family.

This is the book where the scouts finally reveal the secrets of outdoor cooking. Learn them, and gain a skill you'll have for life. Then teach them to someone else. Better still, become a scout (yes, adults can join too) and be part of one of the greatest adventures ever!

BEAR GRYLLS, UK CHIEF SCOUT

GREAT FOOD IN THE GREAT OUTDOORS

When you think back on your camping trip, you'll remember two things – the weather and the food. The weather is not something you can control. But the food is something you can transform into something very special indeed.

In my professional life, as a chef for the Dorchester Collection, I have a team to help me prepare great meals for discerning diners. As a scout leader, I'm sometimes helping 20 scouts cook their first meal. Whatever I'm cooking and whoever I'm cooking with, there are three things that I insist on: good, fresh ingredients, cleanliness and a good cup of tea.

The great outdoors brings a new dimension to food. Whether you're grilling fresh fish on a barbecue, toasting marshmallows over a campfire or stirring a pot on a camping stove, it's simple, back-to-basics cookery. What's more, outdoor cooking is becoming increasingly popular, with the booms in barbecuing, camping, festival-going and surfing all helping to fan the flames.

However, with the myriad of different ways of preparing food outdoors, equipment, legal issues and safety, it can sometimes be baffling. That's why I wanted to write a simple, easy-to-use book on outdoor cooking that's useful to the novice and full of new ideas for the experienced camper.

Scouts have been cooking and eating outdoors since Robert Baden-Powell led the first experimental Scout camp on Brownsea Island in Dorset in 1907. Since then we have devised a vast range of delicious recipes and developed a huge body of expertise in outdoor cooking techniques.

This book distils that expertise into one handy volume, providing a complete reference source for the outdoor cook. From Mexicali Peppers (see page 138) and Baked Chocolate Bananas (see page 160) to Tangy Kebabs (see page 96) and Eggs Cooked in a Potato (see page 58), here are over 80 recipes for barbecues, camping trips, picnics and many other occasions.

I've also asked some of our famous former scouts and supporters to give us their favourite recipes, which I've tested and sampled for myself. From Stephen Fry's Honey Buns (see page 159) to Bear Gryll's Everest Stew (see page 89) – there's a lot of hidden cooking talent out there.

Now it's over to you; happy camping and good luck with your cooking. Let us know how you get on.

Nick Allen

COOKING AND EATING OUTDOORS

So, you've decided to go camping. That's a brave enough step in itself, but now there's a little bit of work ahead. You'll need to choose the right tent, dig out the sleeping bags, book your campsite (checking it's got enough loos and there's a decent pub nearby). But the one thing not to neglect is your food.

Backwoods cooking – cooking without utensils – goes all the way back to the beginnings of Scouting. There is advice in *Scouting for Boys* (published in 1908) on camp cooking, including cooking twists over a fire and how to cook 'Hunter's Stew' (see page 32).

Down the years, scouts have devised hundreds of ingenious ways to prepare, cook and store their food. For someone in the know, an entire kitchen and complete set of utensils can be improvised from little more than the wood lying on the forest floor. Everything from a plate rack to a fork and tongs can be carved, twisted and in use within a couple of hours.

Today cooking is still a huge part of Scouting and the quality of the cooking can make or break a camp. There are badges for all age ranges in Scouting, including the beaver scout healthy eating badge, cub scout chef badge, scout camp cook and survival skills badge.

'COOKING MUST BE EFFICIENT,' SAID SCOUT LEADER PHILIP CARRINGTON IN 1918. 'THE HEALTH, THE TEMPER, THE MORALITY AND THE SUCCESS OF THE CAMP DEPENDS ON REGULAR, GOOD MEALS.'

WHAT'S SO GREAT ABOUT CAMPING ANYWAY?

Camping brings people together. It also makes for great memories. Think about all the holidays and trips you've been on. Which ones do you remember? Chances are it isn't the hotel rooms with little bars of soap and a dry croissant in the morning. It's a small tent at dawn in a field with a flock of migrating birds settling in the next field, the sun climbing in the sky and the prospect of a day stretching out ahead of you. You make your first cup of tea and decide whether you're going to have a swim in the sea or pull on your walking boots and investigate the windmill on the horizon.

Bear Grylls says, 'It doesn't matter whether you're in Kettering or Kathmandu. There's something about spending a night in a tent that restores a great sense of peace and simplicity to your life.' It doesn't cost much, it doesn't take much planning and if you don't like somewhere, you just collapse your tent, pack up your things and move on. Perfect. And have you noticed what happens at campsites? People talk to each other – which isn't something you always see in big towns and cities.

Really, camping is about the outdoors and summer is when the world fully comes to life. When people go away for a weekend's camping in the summer it can sometimes feel much longer. That's because you're spending over 15 hours a day outside. In fact for those who like getting a tan, you're much better off going camping on the south coast of the UK for a couple of days than spending a fortune chasing the sun halfway across the world.

Kids have a right to adventure, and camping with families or Scouting is a great place to start. You don't have to go far to get a completely different view of life. Somehow the world looks more hopeful and exciting when you're peering out of a tent flap instead of a front door.

We are all custodians of planet Earth. This is something we instil in all our scouts. In fact we have a couple of sayings in Scouting when it comes to camping. One is 'leave no trace' – take your rubbish home with you, think about the people, animals and wildlife with whom you are sharing your visit. The other is 'leave nothing behind except your thanks'. But it's not about preaching or telling people how they should behave. Through their activities, scouts acquire a deep understanding and respect for the outdoors. And the best way to appreciate what we have is to get out there and enjoy it. Pack up your car and leave early on a Saturday morning – in a few hours you could be standing on a cliff top watching guillemots and razorbills swoop

'THE ESSENCE AND SPIRIT OF SCOUTING CENTRES ROUND THE CAMPFIRE,' SAID BADEN-POWELL. 'UNTIL YOU HAVE REALISED THE CALL OF THE WILD, UNTIL YOU HAVE GRASPED THE JOY OF THE SCENT OF THE WOOD SMOKE IN YOUR NOSTRILS AND OF THE DEFTNESS OF CAMPER-CRAFT IN YOUR FINGER TIPS, THEN A TROOP OF SO-CALLED SCOUTS IS LITTLE MORE THAN A DRILL BRIGADE.'

and dive around you, or swim in a lake. You can very quickly be surrounded by birds and animals you've never seen before and people you've never met.

Camping is on the increase at the moment. Why? Well, maybe because it's cheap. But I think there's a more important reason than that. I think more people are camping – and why Scouting is growing for that matter – because people want more out of life. They're not getting it going to the shops. Going camping teaches you things about yourself; it reminds you that we depend on each other to get by and that some of the most precious things in life are friendships, the natural world and reaching our potential.

'Stay dry!' recommends UK chief scout Bear Grylls. 'It doesn't matter how hot or cold it is, if you don't stay dry, chances are you'll be miserable. Make sure you take a ground mat with you to sleep on and keep your kit away from the sides of the tent. If you get wet, get out of those clothes straight away. Borrow someone else's clothes if you have to – that's all part of the fun!'

THERE IS NO INTERNATIONAL COOKERY COURT THAT WILL TAKE YOU TO TASK IF YOU BREAK THE RULES. **SO DO WHAT YOU LIKE.** JUST REMEMBER THESE BASIC PRINCIPLES: **DON'T BOIL OR STEW MEAT HARD OR FAST.** FRY THINGS AS HOT AND FAST AS YOU CAN (EXCEPTION: SCRAMBLED EGGS). **DON'T FORGET THE SALT AND PEPPER.** DON'T LEAVE A DRY BILLY CAN OVER THE FIRE: IT WILL BURN!

OUTDOOR
COOKING

PLANNING
YOUR CAMP KITCHEN

■ Think carefully about where you locate your kitchen. It should be as near as possible to the water supply and downwind of the main camp so that the prevailing wind takes away odours from the kitchen and smoke from the fire, without crossing the working areas.

■ Make sure it is on level ground.

■ A fire shelter is essential.

■ You will also need to make provision for covering the preparation table, wood pile and serving table in the event of wet weather.

Dish cloths (6)   Buckets   Hatchet   Soda   Felling axe

Milk jug   2 Pudding cloths   Pudding basins   Knife fork & spoon

6 Gallons   2 Gallons   2 Basins   Plates

2 Frying pans   2 Mugs   KITCHEN EQUIPMENT

FIRES

OR STOVES?

Food is not cooked by equipment, but by people. More accurately, food is cooked by the correct use of an adequate and constant source of heat. The wood fire or portable stove is, therefore, the most important aspect of the kitchen and cooking arrangements. The wood fire has always been a popular means of cooking, but fuel supplies or sites that allow wood fires can be increasingly difficult to find.

Camping stoves of various types are becoming more popular and, therefore, the traditional approach to camp cooking is changing. Both wood fires and portable (pressure or gas) stoves have their advantages and disadvantages, so you will need to decide which is appropriate for your situation.

Wood fires are generally better:

When large numbers are being catered for.

For camps lasting more than two nights on the same site.

For food with a cooking time of more than about 30 minutes.

When part of the purpose of the camp is to encourage the understanding of different cooking techniques.

Portable (pressure gas) stoves are generally better:

When cooking for small numbers.

For hiking and backpacking.

When there is no wood available on the site.

When all you want is a quick cup of tea or speed is essential.

In poor weather conditions.

If you are fed up with being blinded by wood smoke!

OPEN FIRES

Building and lighting an open fire is a vital skill for any outdoor cook. You will need it for cooking and keeping warm. Before you start to build a fire, you will need to think carefully about its location. You might also have to use an altar fire (see page 20) if you are not allowed to build it on the ground. You will need a good supply of wood.

Fires need three things to burn: fuel (wood), oxygen (which is in the air) and heat. If you take away any of these three, your fire will go out.

Natural tinder

If you're going to start a fire from scratch, you're going to need some light material to catch that first spark. Here are five natural tinders:

Cramp ball – look for these on dead ash trees. They are great used with a fire steel or fire piston, and you can cook over them too.

Birch bark – peel off thin strips and place them in a bundle. Ignite with a fire steel.

Amadou (horse hoof fungus) – found on beech and birch trees. Use the leathery insides with a fire steel for best results.

Punk wood – dry, rotten wood that falls apart when handled. Works well in a fire piston.

Cattail (bulrush) – often found by wetlands. Fluff up the heads and use to take a spark, or add to a bow drill ember.

Pine resin – smear onto something dry and fibrous, and ignite with a fire steel.

Choosing your firewood

Not all wood burns well. The chart opposite will help identify and guide you to finding the better woods for lighting and burning.

WOODS FOR BURNING

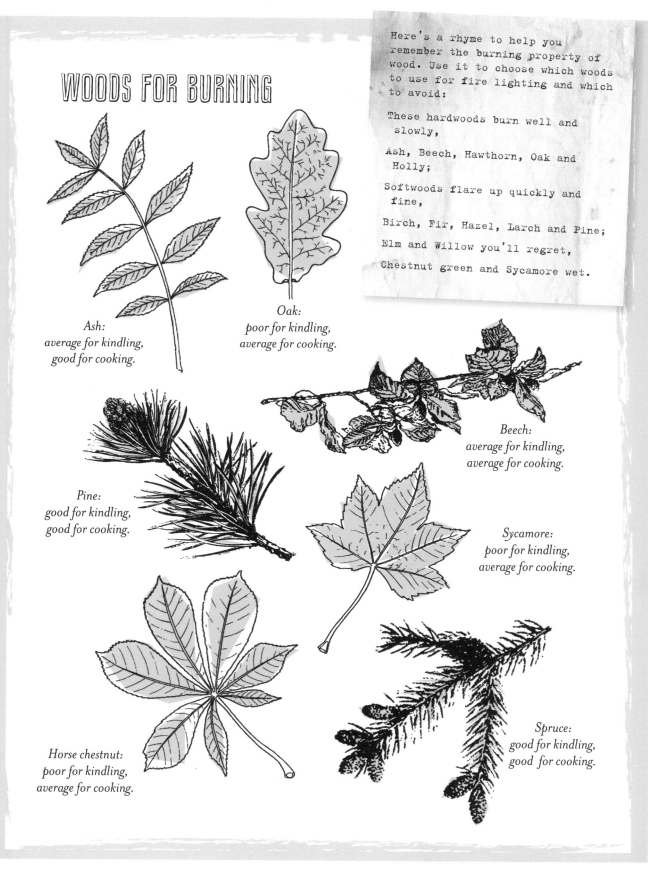

Here's a rhyme to help you remember the burning property of wood. Use it to choose which woods to use for fire lighting and which to avoid:

These hardwoods burn well and slowly,

Ash, Beech, Hawthorn, Oak and Holly;

Softwoods flare up quickly and fine,

Birch, Fir, Hazel, Larch and Pine;

Elm and Willow you'll regret,

Chestnut green and Sycamore wet.

Ash:
average for kindling,
good for cooking.

Oak:
poor for kindling,
average for cooking.

Beech:
average for kindling,
average for cooking.

Pine:
good for kindling,
good for cooking.

Sycamore:
poor for kindling,
average for cooking.

Horse chestnut:
poor for kindling,
average for cooking.

Spruce:
good for kindling,
good for cooking.

BUILDING YOUR FIRE

There are many different types of fire you can use. Here are some examples:

Altar fire

Some campsites do not allow fires on the ground. Altar fires can be made out of metal, or can be built from logs. The logs are placed in opposite directions to one another. The top layer is then covered in mud. This stops the logs catching alight and makes a good base for the fire.

Star fire

A star fire is built using three main logs. The three logs are placed together to form a star shape. A small fire is started in the middle and as the logs burn, they are moved towards the centre.

Trench fire

To make a trench fire, you need to dig a trench or pit. You may want to place a screen of logs or stones along the side to shield you from the heat. The fire is built in the trench.

Building and lighting a pyramid fire

1 Stand the first twig upright in the ground and surround it with tinder or punk. Build a wigwam shape by surrounding the first twig with kindling.

2 Use progressively thicker twigs, expanding the shape and leaving a gap at the bottom for your fire.

3 Light a match, shielding the flame in your hand and getting as near as possible to the wood.

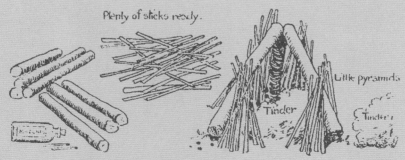

Plenty of sticks ready.

Little pyramids

Tinder

Tinder

4 Light the tinder or punk and any small pieces of kindling first. Add more twigs as necessary to each flame until it spreads to thicker wood.

5 If you need to blow the fire, get in close and blow gently.

6 Once alight, add larger and larger twigs and sticks. Then add a few pieces of wood at one end so that they catch light. When these are well lit, add more wood to the other end.

7 When it is firmly established, and the wigwam shape has been abandoned, lay bricks or thick logs parallel with the wind direction on either side of the fire.

8 If you intend to cook, you will have to wait until there are hot, glowing embers as this is where the heat is retained.

The art of firelighting

My suggestion is to go back to 'ordinary' methods of firelighting using matches or even lighters.

Fuel needs to be graded and to be added at the right moment. Learn the art of finding sources of dry tinder in a wet wood; most people are familiar with the wonderful burning ability of Silver Birch bark, but what if there are no birch trees around? Try searching the dead branches of conifers that are below the shelter of the living green fronds further up. Also, try splitting damp logs that are not lying on the floor; very often these are dry enough for early fuel on a fire.

It is important to prepare further stocks of fuel. Piling logs up will 'reflect heat' and will also dry out the wood. In addition, dry smaller tinder over the fire so that you have a good supply.

Putting out the fire

You should always make sure that any fire you have lit is out before you leave it. You can use water to help.

Never leave a fire unattended.

Keep a bucket of water, sand or earth next to the fire.

DON'T FORGET!

• You will need to light a fire at least 30 minutes before you intend to cook on it. You should never cook on roaring flames as these give an intense but fluctuating heat. Instead, wait until you are left with glowing embers – similar to barbecue coals – before starting to cook.

• Whenever you leave the site or retire to bed, ensure that the fire is completely out or is in a safe condition to avoid the chances of it spreading.

• Leave the fireplace as you found it, so that there is no trace that you have been there.

• Have ready a bucket of water, sand or earth and a spade should you need to put out the fire in an emergency.

• If the earth is wet, build your fire on top of a sheet of aluminium foil placed on the ground.

OVENS

You won't find many places to plug in a microwave in the great outdoors – and who needs one of those anyway? Scouts have devised ways to create their own ovens from natural materials. Here are some of the most popular.

THE CARDBOARD OVEN

These ovens are fun to make and use.

You will need

1 x strong cardboard box (ones that contain wine bottles are usually very rigid)

Masking tape

A roll of wide cooking foil

A wire cooling rack (or similar)

4 x metal tent pegs

An abundance of patience!

REFLECTOR OVEN

A reflector oven uses a reflective surface like a thin sheet of metal near a fire to create a hotter environment, just like an oven.

Method

1 Carefully remove and set aside the top and bottom of the box, using a sharp knife.

2 Taking a lot of care, completely cover the inside and outside of the box with foil, using masking tape on the outside to secure it. To do this, you will need to lay your strips of foil on the inside so that 15 cm (6 inches) of foil sticks out at the top and bottom of the box. This can then be folded over and fixed in place on the outside. NB: The foil must *completely* cover the insides.

3 Top the box with the piece of cardboard to make a lid.

4 Make a shelf by pushing the four metal pegs through the corners of the box and then rest the wire cake-cooler upon these supports. The shelf should be supported about 15 cm (6 inches) above the ground.

5 Dig a shallow pit the same width and length as the box, and light a good fire in it – or use charcoal for best results.

6 When the glowing embers form, place the cardboard oven above the coals, with your food on the shelf inside it. Put the lid on top and secure it all in place with stones.

Once your oven is up and running, there's a ream of tasty dishes that can be tried at camp. Roll homemade pizzas to fit in your oven, get traditional with toad in the hole or sweeten up with a selection of fruit pies and crumbles.

METAL BOX OVEN

This is a simple construction that offers really good cooking results. It is comprised of a metal box (a biscuit tin works well for small ovens) placed over a fire. Larger ovens can be made out of an oil drum. Care must be taken to ensure it is cleaned out properly before you cook in it. To make a large oven the following instructions should be followed:

You will need

1 x metal container (size according to your needs) — anything from a biscuit tin up to an oil drum is suitable

Several tall thin metal tins or a metal/clay drainpipe

The lid of the container or a metal sheet.

Method

1 Find a bank and dig a hole or a trench in it.

2 Rest your metal container in the top of the hole in the bank or over the trench.

3 Build and light a fire underneath and pile earth or clay over and around the oven on two sides. Be wary of flints or stones that may explode.

4 Make a chimney from tall thin tins, or a metal/clay drainpipe at the back and pile the earth around it.

5 Use the lid of the container or a suitable metal sheet as the oven door. A grid can be inserted into the oven to make a shelf and will stop the food burning on the bottom.

HAYBOX OVEN

The trick to haybox cooking (also called retained-heat cooking) is not in the making of the heat, but creating an insulated environment that enables partially cooked food to continue cooking slowly in its own heat without needing to add fuel. Depending on the type and amount of food, the use of a haybox or insulated cooker could save between 20–80 percent of the energy normally needed to cook food. The principle of haybox cooking is simple. Since any heat applied to a pot after it reaches boiling point functions to replace heat lost to the air by the pot, when the cooker is insulated, most of the heat in the food is prevented from escaping into the environment. Thus no additional energy is needed to complete the cooking process.

The haybox oven works best for cooking casseroles, rice and porridge but ensure that you are not rushed for time as the cooking time is roughly twice as long as the normal time it would take to prepare a meal. A good idea is to partially cook the food (method described on page 24) just after the last meal, and it should be ready in time for the next one.

You will need

A solid wooden box, for example a tea chest, or a hole in the ground (any insulated container that can withstand cooking temperatures and fits snugly around the pot will do. Since hot air rises, a container that opens at the base rather than the top will retain more heat)

Cotton sheeting and a pillowcase

Insulating material: either hay or polystyrene beads, newspaper torn into shreds and rolled into small balls, straw, wool, feathers, cotton, rice hulls, cardboard, aluminium foil and/or other suitable insulating materials (ensure the material does not release any toxic fumes or fibres so be aware of fibreglass and foams)

Sheets of newspaper to line the box

A cooking pot

Method

1 Line the bottom and the sides of the box with layers of newspaper.

2 Place thick layers of hay in the bottom of the box and fill up to halfway. Press down firmly.

3 Select a pot with a tightly fitting lid and stand it in the centre of the box on top of the hay.

4 Pack more hay or other insulating material around the pot, approximately 4–10 cm (2–4 inches) of thickness, and up to the rim. Make sure you can still lift the pot easily from the hay.

5 Remove the pot and line the nest with old cotton sheeting to prevent bits of hay getting into the pot.

6 Pack the rest of the hay into a cotton pillowcase and fit it snugly on top of the lid.

7 Cover the box with a piece of wood or board to create a heat trap.

8 Follow the same method when using a hole in the ground. However, one should line the hole with plastic sheeting first to ensure that the ground moisture does not dampen the newspaper.

How to prepare food for cooking in a haybox oven

1 Prepare the stew or casserole, as you would usually do on a stove, but ensure that the pot is as full as possible.

2 Bring the dish to the boil and simmer for a few minutes depending on the size of the ingredients you are using (5 minutes for rice or other grains, 15 minutes for large dry beans or whole potatoes). It is about one-third of the overall cooking time.

3 Quickly transfer the pot to the haybox (see above), while still boiling, for the remaining two-thirds of the cooking time.

4 When ready to eat, remove the pot from the haybox and bring back to the boil, stirring occasionally to ensure the entire dish is heated through. Serve immediately.

HAWAIIAN OVEN

Also known as a pit, underground or earth oven, this is a method of cooking that was traditionally used in Polynesia and the Americas. The cabbage leaves are used to create steam and the cooking is therefore a form of steaming rather than the dry heat of a regular oven. Originally, coconut palm leaves, banana leaves or honhono grass was used instead. The real art is figuring out how long to leave your food cooking, which is determined by the type and weight of your food. It is really all a case of trial and error.

You will need

A hole in the ground, 60 cm (2 ft) deep by about 30 cm (1 ft) square.

A number of washed stones

1 x large cabbage

Method

1 Light a good fire in the hole and when the flames have died down and you are left with a large quantity of hot embers, lay the stones on top of the hot coals.

2 Carefully place 2 or 3 layers of cabbage leaves on top of the stones and place the prepared food on top of the leaves.

3 Cover the food with another 3 layers of leaves and cover that with earth, ensuring that no steam or smoke escapes from the hole.

4 The food will take about 5 or 6 hours to cook so it is a good idea to prepare the oven and the food in the morning of a busy day, so that when you return to camp in the evening, your oven will be piping hot and ready for you.

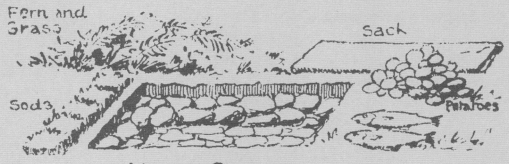

MAORI OVEN

THE IDEAL SCOUT CAN LIVE ON A DESERT ISLAND WITH A PEN-KNIFE AND A TOMAHAWK.

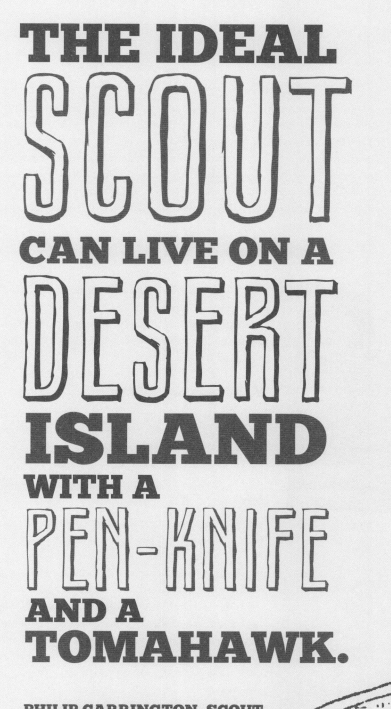

PHILIP CARRINGTON, SCOUT
LEADER AND AUTHOR, 1918

CAMPING STOVES

What your outdoor kitchen looks like will depend very much on the number of mouths to feed and the number of meals you will be preparing. If you are just camping solo for an evening then a lightweight stove such as a Trangia is ideal; for a family or larger group then more robust equipment is required. Shop around and don't be afraid to ask for assistance – the chances are that the people running your local camping shop will be keen campers themselves. Make sure you practise in your garden and in good weather before setting out on your expedition. Learning how to use your stove in the dark while it's raining is never a good idea.

Amount of heat

If you're just going to be cooking for two or three people then a spirit burner like a Trangia will be fine, and you might even get away with a tiny hexamine stove. If you're cooking more complicated things, or cooking for larger numbers of people, then you'll be better with a more powerful stove.

Weight and portability

For a fixed camp then the traditional Primus or suitcase-style petrol stove with multiple burners are good. If you're moving around and carrying your cooking equipment with you then you'll need something lighter.

Fuel

Some fuels are more expensive than others, or more difficult to get hold of. Gas stoves are light and very easy to use, but you might not always be able to get canisters that fit. Trangia fuel is cheap and widely available. Multi-fuels are very adaptable, and can give out good heat, but check product reviews before you buy, as they are expensive and can be temperamental. Remember too that some fuels don't work well in low temperatures. If you're camping with young people, it's also worth bearing in mind that some fuels are more dangerous than others. Pressurised petrol stoves can be particularly hazardous.

DUTCH OVEN COOKING

With a bit of practice (and some patience), pretty much anything you can cook in a normal oven or over a hob can be cooked outdoors in a Dutch oven.

The method of using a Dutch oven has been around for hundreds of years. They are traditionally thick cast-iron pots with lids and commonly with handles. The familiar shape historically comes from the Baltic regions of Europe but have been produced in England since 1710. The advantages of using a Dutch oven are that it is perfect for long slow cooking processes as it retains its heat due to the cast iron.

How to cook chicken in a Dutch oven

To cook chicken, allow about 25 minutes per 500 g (1 lb). Get the oven up to temperature using charcoal (briquettes or lumpwood) distributed evenly underneath the pot and on top of the lid. To the chicken, add about a 300 ml)½ pint) water, a chicken stock cube and some salt and pepper, then put the lid on.

To keep an even heat, it can be a good idea to rotate your oven. Try turning the pot one-third of a revolution clockwise every 15 minutes or so, and turning the lid about the same distance anti-clockwise.

About 30 minutes before you think the chicken will be ready, add some new potatoes, then about 15 minutes after that some carrots and broccoli. Wait a few more minutes and you should have delicious cooked chicken with all the trimmings. Just be sure to check it's all cooked right through and that the chicken juices run clear.

GET A PRESSURE COOKER!

I am a great believer that with a little forethought and planning there is very little you can cook in a conventional kitchen that can't be cooked in a camp kitchen or on a campfire. I have seen pictures of American scouts using metal mailboxes as ovens on a campfire. In our troop, we have been experimenting with a pressure cooker, with some excellent results.

Used in the standard way a pressure cooker is very efficient, therefore requiring less time and using less fuel than conventional saucepans. At camp we cooked beef stew and dumplings on a gas burner from start to finish in 40 minutes.

You will need

225 g (7½ oz/1 cup) bread flour

1 x 7-g sachet active dried yeast

1 teaspoon salt

Flour, for dusting

RECESSION BUSTER

Your pressure cooker doesn't have to be new – we picked ours up for a small amount at a car boot sale.

How to make bread using your pressure cooker

1 Put the dry ingredients in a bowl and add enough water to make a firm elastic dough. Once the dough is mixed, tip onto a lightly floured surface and knead for 5 minutes. Shape and put into your tin. At this stage, it should come about halfway up the side. Cover and leave to rise. The bread is ready to cook when the dough is about 2 cm (just under 1 inch) above the rim of the tin.

2 Put an upturned saucer in the bottom of the pressure cooker and pour in water to a depth of about 2.5 cm (1 inch). Place the tin on the saucer, put the lid on and seal it. Bring to pressure and cook for about 20 minutes. The bread comes out somewhat like a boiled sponge pudding and of course it is not crusty, but our scouts scoffed the lot, so that doesn't matter much!

(With thanks to Jo Lawson, assistant scout leader, Amberley scout group, Gloucestershire)

How to make stew using your pressure cooker

Put the stew together as normal. Place the pressure cooker on the heat and bring up to pressure, then cook the stew for 30 minutes. This method was just the ticket after spending the day cutting down vegetation at the side of a steam railway line. Pressure cooker stew is best with lamb and beef, but also works with chicken. If you're using dark meat increase the cooking time by about 15 minutes.

COOKING METHODS

Everyone would soon get fed up if they had to eat the same food cooked the same way every day, but most foods can be cooked in a number of different ways, each with its own end result in terms of taste and texture. Cooking times vary, however (always check with a recipe if you are unsure how long to cook something for).

When using a variety of methods, take care to check that the food is well cooked (that is, not still raw!) and that all parts of the dish are ready to be served at the same time.

Many foods benefit from the addition of herbs or sauces, and you should not be afraid to use them just because you are at camp. There is little excuse for bland, tasteless food to be served. Here are some of the different methods or cooking techniques that can be used:

VARYING THE COOKING METHOD

Most of the recipes in this book give a basic method of how to cook over a campfire. Please don't feel restricted by this, and feel free to change the cooking method to suit you and your camp.

Remember to adjust the cooking times depending on the method you use – a barbecue will cook quicker and in a more controlled way than using a campfire; using a camp oven will increase the cooking time, especially if you add on the building time!

Boiling – cooking in water ('It's boiling when it's bubbling'!)

This is the simplest and most common method of cooking and, providing you don't boil the pot dry, the method least likely to go wrong! This method may be used for most vegetables, rice and pasta, and cooking periods range from about 10 minutes from the time the water comes to the boil for green vegetables, to 30 minutes for the harder root vegetables such as carrots. Root vegetables should be placed in the water and brought to the boil from cold; greens are best put into the water once it has boiled. All vegetables should be cooked with the pot lids on, but pasta is boiled without a lid. Take care not to overcook as all foods tend to lose colour, taste, texture and nutritional value if boiled for too long.

Stewing – cooking in water below boiling point

This is the term used for bringing food to boiling point, and then simmering it at a temperature just below boiling point without letting it bubble furiously. An old saying, 'a stew boiled is a stew spoiled' sums it up very well! It is normally used as a means of cooking meat or fruit. In the case of meat, at least an hour is required after the liquid comes to the boil. Root vegetables are normally included in a meat stew, but the softer ones, such as potatoes must be

ROBERT
BADEN-POWELL'S
ORIGINAL RECIPE **NUMBER 1**

HUNTER'S
STEW

CHOP YOUR MEAT INTO SMALL CHUNKS ABOUT ONE INCH OR ONE AND A HALF INCHES SQUARE. SCRAPE AND CHOP UP ANY VEGETABLES, SUCH AS POTATOES, CARROTS AND ONIONS, AND PUT THEM INTO YOUR 'BILLY'.

ADD CLEAN WATER OR SOUP UNTIL IT IS HALF FULL. MIX SOME FLOUR, SALT AND PEPPER TOGETHER AND RUB YOUR MEAT WELL IN IT, AND PUT THIS IN THE 'BILLY'. THERE SHOULD BE ENOUGH WATER JUST TO COVER THE FOOD – NO MORE. LET THE BILLY STAND IN THE EMBERS AND SIMMER FOR ABOUT ONE HOUR AND A QUARTER. THE POTATOES TAKE LONGEST TO COOK. WHEN THESE ARE SOFT (WHICH YOU SHOULD TRY WITH A FORK) ENOUGH NOT TO LIFT OUT, THE WHOLE STEW IS COOKED.

TAKEN FROM 'SCOUTING FOR BOYS', 1908

added part way through the cooking to avoid overcooking them and reducing them to pulp. Meat stews need the addition of stock cubes, and there is also a wide range of powdered sauce mixes, which can make a great difference. Sugar has to be added to all stewed fruit. For any stew, long simmering times require good fire management.

Frying – cooking over heat with a film of fat covering the bottom of the pan

This is often assumed to be the most common method of cooking at camp; in fact it is the most difficult cooking method to do well. The main problem is maintaining a moderate heat source over a large enough cooking area to allow more than two or three people to be served together. A fire can provide a large enough cooking area, but it can be difficult to hold the critical temperature needed for more than a few minutes. Stoves have a flame that can be more readily controlled over a period of time, but burners are rarely large enough to cook in large quantities. Frying, and hence the use of fat, has had a bad press in recent years on health grounds, and is best used sparingly.

Stir-frying – cooking quickly over a high heat

This has the advantage of cooking all of the ingredients – meat and vegetables – in the same pan at the same time. Therefore it has considerable potential for camp use as it reduces the space required over fires, takes less time compared to other methods, and it can be prepared and served together. Care will, however, need to be taken to perhaps start certain ingredients before others such as meat before vegetables as their overall cooking time is different.

Deep frying – cooking by complete immersion in hot fat or oil is more difficult and can be dangerous in a camp situation, but can be done

This method may be used for cooking food such as fish and vegetables coated in batter or breadcrumbs.

Baking – cooking in an oven without covering and roasting or cooking in an oven with fat is feasible in a camp oven constructed from a biscuit tin or similar metal box encased in clay and fitted with a chimney (see page 23)

This arrangement allows the heat from a fire burning in a trench underneath to completely surround the oven and give a very good result. No calibration is possible, however, and cooking times must be determined by trial and error! Baking can be used for most foods from pastry and bread to meat and vegetables. Potatoes can be baked, wrapped in foil and placed in the glowing embers that are left after the flames have died down in a fire. Roasting is generally used for meat and vegetables.

Pot-roasting – a method of roasting a joint of meat without an oven

An ideal container is a large billy can, with a capacity of 7–8 litres (12–13 pints) and a diameter of about 20 cm (8 inches). Hard root vegetables such as turnips, swedes and parsnips are cut into large pieces (onions are best left whole), packed tightly into the bottom of the billy to a depth of about 10 cm (4 inches), and just covered with water. The meat is then placed on top of the vegetables, standing clear of the liquid. The billy is brought to the boil and simmered with a lid on until the meat is tender – this normally takes about 30 minutes per 500 g (1 lb), depending on the cut. The billy must be checked regularly during cooking to make sure it does not boil dry.

Grilling – cooking over or under a direct and fierce heat

This method is appropriate for thin cuts of meat, fish, poultry or game, a few vegetables such as mushrooms and tomatoes and bread (for toast). This is a relatively quick method of cooking which should not be left unattended as food will often need 'turning' during cooking. A barbecue works on this principle.

ROBERT
BADEN-POWELL'S
ORIGINAL RECIPE **NUMBER 2**

BREAD

TO MAKE BREAD, THE USUAL WAY IS FOR A SCOUT TO TAKE OFF HIS COAT, SPREAD IT ON THE GROUND, WITH THE INSIDE UPPERMOST (SO THAT ANY MESS HE MAKES IN IT WILL NOT SHOW OUTWARDLY WHEN HE WEARS HIS COAT AFTERWARDS); THEN HE MAKES A PILE OF FLOUR ON THE COAT AND SCOOPS OUT THE CENTRE UNTIL IT FORMS A CUP FOR THE WATER WHICH HE THEN POURS IN HOT; HE THEN MIXES THE DOUGH WITH A PINCH OR TWO OF SALT, AND OF BAKING POWER, AND KNEADS AND MIXES IT WELL TOGETHER UNTIL IT FORMS A LUMP OF WELL MIXED DOUGH. THEN, WITH A LITTLE FRESH FLOUR SPRINKLED OVER THE HANDS TO PREVENT THE DOUGH STICKING TO THEM, HE PATS IT AND MAKES IT INTO THE SHAPE OF A LARGE BUN OR SEVERAL BUNS.

THEN HE PUTS IT ON A GRIDIRON OVER HOT ASHES OR SWEEPS PART OF THE FIRE TO ONE SIDE AND ON THE HOT GROUND LEFT THERE HE PUTS HIS DOUGH AND PILES HOT ASHES AROUND IT AND LETS IT BAKE ITSELF. ONLY SMALL LOAVES LIKE BUNS CAN BE MADE IN THIS WAY.

TAKEN FROM 'SCOUTING FOR BOYS', 1908

Poaching – cooking food in simmering water

The water is boiled and then kept simmering at just below boiling point. This method is suitable for eggs and fish. Eggs can be done individually by breaking them onto a plate or saucer and then sliding them into the simmering water. With the help of two spoons cover the yolks with the white of the eggs. The pan should then be covered and the eggs allowed to cook for 5–6 minutes. For fish, cover with lightly salted water and leave to simmer until it flakes easily, allowing about 10 minutes for 500 g (1 lb) of fish.

Steaming – cooking in the steam resulting from boiling water

This can be used for fish, poultry, vegetables or puddings. Steaming can be done by one of two methods: firstly, by placing a small amount of water in a saucepan with a tightly fitting lid and by keeping it 'on the boil' the resulting steam cooks the food; or, secondly, by using a specifically designed 'steamer'. The timing varies considerably depending upon what is being cooked – for example, fillets or thin cuts of fish will take about 10–15 minutes, a whole chicken, 3–4 hours, vegetables about 5 minutes longer than boiling them and puddings take between 2–3 hours. For both methods, you need to check that they don't 'boil dry'.

Braising – cooking in an oven in a tightly closed container

This method, like pot-roasting, is a slow method and therefore requires more planning. It can be used for meat (smaller cuts of meat rather than a joint), fish, poultry, game and vegetables.

ROBERT
BADEN-POWELL'S

ORIGINAL RECIPE **NUMBER 3**

KABOBS

CUT YOUR MEAT UP INTO SLICES ABOUT THREE OR THREE-QUARTERS OF AN INCH THICK; CUT THIS UP INTO SMALL PIECES ABOUT ONE TO ONE AND A HALF INCHES ACROSS. STRING A LOT OF THESE CHUNKS ON TO A STICK OR IRON ROD AND PLANT IT IN FRONT OF THE FIRE, OR SUSPEND IT OVER THE HOT EMBERS FOR A FEW MINUTES TILL THE MEAT IS ROASTED.

TAKEN FROM 'SCOUTING FOR BOYS', 1908

MEASURING QUANTITIES AT CAMP

We take measuring ingredients at home for granted as we have the equipment that will do the job. However, at camp, we may be limited in what equipment is available. All of the recipes in this book provide the standard metric and imperial measurements, but they also include a standard camp mug measurement so that you can easily measure your ingredients without having to take scales with you.

Here are a few hints on what can be used:

25 g (1 oz) flour, cocoa, custard powder = 1 well-heaped tablespoon.

25 g (1 oz) sugar, rice, butter, fat = 1 level tablespoon.

250 ml (8 fl oz) liquid = 1 normal camp mug.

It is possible to use a camp mug for measuring all sorts of things. For example, when lightly filled, it will hold the following approximate weights:

125 g (4 oz) flour

200 g (7 oz) sugar

100 g (3½ oz) grated cheese

175 g (6 oz) rice

150 g (5 oz) dried fruit

Wherever possible, of course, ingredients can be prepared or weighed at home before leaving for camp, or other containers can be checked for how much they will hold if you haven't got a standard camp mug to take with you.

TOP CAMP COOKING TIPS

■ Always wash your hands before handling food.

■ Keep the insides of cooking utensils scrupulously clean.

■ If you use frozen food, ensure that it is completely thawed before use.

■ If frying on a wood fire, use a covered frying pan or splatter guard.

■ If you are using a portable stove, make sure that you have enough fuel before you start cooking.

■ If you are using a wood fire, ensure that the grid will take the weight of the utensils safely.

■ If you are using a wood fire, make sure that you light it in plenty of time – it's not like switching on an oven.

■ The best cooking fires are not only smokeless but also virtually flameless. A good bed of hot ashes gives a constant heat – and constant heat is the secret of good cooking.

■ If you are using a wood fire, coat the outside of cooking utensils with detergent before using – it makes them much easier to clean afterwards.

■ Keep a container of hot water on the fire or stove whenever you are working in the camp kitchen – you will always have an instant supply for washing-up water and cups of tea.

■ Always stoke up the fire under the washing-up water before you sit down to eat.

■ Do not attempt to lift heavy containers of boiling water – to transfer water, use a jug or ladle to avoid scalds.

■ Handles of cooking utensils can become very hot – use oven gloves or pads to avoid burns.

■ Serve your food in an attractive and appetising way. Even something which tastes 'perfect' can be off-putting if not presented well.

■ Keep the kitchen area tidy if you want to be able to find everything when you want it.

■ Burn or bin food scraps immediately after every meal.

■ When removed, lids of cooking utensils should always be put down rim uppermost.

■ Serving spoons, ladles and other cooking implements should be put on a plate – never on the ground.

■ Finally, remember, 'too many cooks spoil the broth'!

YOU CAN TELL A SCOUT'S CHARACTER BY THE NUMBER OF CURRANTS HE PUTS IN HIS PORRIDGE.

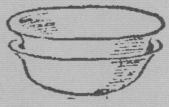

PHILIP CARRINGTON, SCOUT
LEADER AND AUTHOR, 1918

ENJOYING GREAT
OUTDOOR FOOD SHOULD
NOT BE RESTRICTED TO
MEALTIMES. HERE ARE
SOME DELICIOUS NIBBLES,
SNACKS AND LIGHT BITES,
USING INTERNATIONAL
FLAVOURS ALONG
WITH SOME SCOUTING
CLASSICS.

SNACKS
AND LIGHT
BITES

MOROCCAN FLATBREAD
WITH HOMEMADE TZATZIKI

SERVES 6

500 g (1 lb/4 cups) strong white flour, plus extra for dusting

2 tablespoons salt

1 teaspoon ground cumin

3 tablespoons olive oil

7-g sachet of quick-action yeast

300 ml (½ pint/1 and a bit cups) warm water

Butter, for greasing

FOR THE TZATZIKI

250 g (10 oz/1 cup) natural yogurt

½ cucumber, deseeded and grated

1 garlic clove, crushed

20 fresh mint leaves, finely chopped

Salt and pepper

There's only one problem with Moroccan food – it's very moreish!

1 Make the tzatziki. Mix all of the ingredients together in a bowl, add some seasoning and chill in a cool box until needed.

2 Mix the flour, salt, cumin, olive oil and yeast together in a bowl and then add the warm water a little at a time, until a soft, but not wet dough is formed.

3 Leave the dough in a greased bowl covered with cling film for about 30 minutes until it has doubled in size.

4 Turn the dough out onto a double layer of foil that has been lightly dusted with flour and roll it out using a rolling pin or clean empty wine bottle until it is about 1 cm (½ inch) thick. Snip it into small pieces (triangles or rectangles for example) using scissors, depending on how many you are catering for.

5 Cook the flatbreads directly on a hot barbecue grill for about 1–2 minutes on each side (or until they have puffed up slightly and have a hollow sound when tapped). Alternatively, lay a single sheet of foil directly onto the glowing campfire embers and cook the flatbreads on top for the same amount of time.

 BE PREPARED Make the flatbread dough at home before going on camp. Keep it well wrapped and then roll out and cook on your barbecue or campfire.

I CAN LIGHT A
FIRE
WITH TWO STICKS
AS LONG AS
ONE OF THEM IS A
MATCH.

OLD JOKE

ROASTED POTATO WEDGES
WITH SMOKED PAPRIKA

SERVES 6

8 potatoes (Maris Piper or
   King Edwards work best),
   peeled or skin left on as
   preferred
A drizzle of olive oil, plus
   extra for greasing
1 teaspoon smoked paprika
Salt and pepper

This is probably the closest you will come to a chip in this book, so make the most of it. The paprika brings just a little bit of colour and flavour to the common or garden spud.

1 Cut the potatoes into wedges, about 8–12 per potato.

2 Put the wedges on a greased double layer of foil. Coat the potatoes with a little olive oil, season with salt and pepper and then sprinkle with the smoked paprika. Fold the foil around the wedges and seal into a parcel.

3 Place the foil parcel directly on the glowing campfire embers and bake for 40–60 minutes. Shake the foil parcel halfway through the cooking time.

TRY SOMETHING DIFFERENT

• Cook the potato wedges in a frying pan directly over the campfire embers.

• The potatoes could also be laid out on a greased baking tray and cooked in a prepared camp oven (see pages 22-5) -just add 10-15 minutes to the cooking time.

a 15-cm (6-inch) length of French bread or
half a baguette
50 g (2 oz/¼ cup) butter or margarine
Half a crushed garlic clove or a pinch of
powdered garlic or garlic salt

GARLIC BREAD

This is a much cheaper and tastier version of the shop-
bought variety. Add 25 g (1 oz/¼ cup) cheese to the
mixture if you prefer your garlic bread cheesy.

1 Make deep cuts in the bread at 2.5-cm (1-inch) intervals, making
sure that you do not cut through the bottom crust. Open up the cuts
slightly to make room for the butter or margarine, taking care again
not to break the bottom crust.

2 Mix the butter or margarine with the garlic and spread it generously
into the cuts in the bread.

3 Press the slices in the bread back together and wrap loosely in a
double layer of foil.

4 Place the foil parcel directly on the glowing campfire embers for
about 15 minutes, turning regularly.

TRY SOMETHING DIFFERENT

• Lay the asparagus on a greased double layer of foil, seal into a parcel and place directly on the glowing campfire embers or in a prepared camp oven (see pages 22-5) and cook for the same amount of time.

• Cook the asparagus in a frying pan over a high heat on a camp stove for the same amount of time.

SERVES 4

12 asparagus spears
A drizzle of olive oil
100 ml (3½ fl oz/½ cup) crème fraîche
100 g (3½ oz/1 cup) soft blue cheese (such as
  Dolcelatte)
1 tablespoon finely chopped chives
Salt and pepper

QUICK GRILLED ASPARAGUS
WITH BLUE CHEESE DIP

If you don't like cheese, then move on! Asparagus and blue cheese work brilliantly together but are not often paired up. Now is the time to start.

1 Trim the asparagus to about 10 cm (4 inches) in length, or let it naturally snap when you bend it to remove the woody end.

2 Coat the asparagus with a drizzle of oil and seasoning and place the spears directly onto a hot barbecue grill.

3 Keep turning the spears and cook them until slightly wrinkled and tender to the touch, about 8–10 minutes.

4 Meanwhile, mix the crème fraîche and soft blue cheese together in a bowl, mashing it with the back of a spoon until combined and smooth and creamy. Top with the chopped chives.

5 Dip your asparagus into the cheese dip while still warm.

NETTLE AND WILD GARLIC SOUP

SERVES 4

400 g (13 oz/2 cups) nettle
   leaves
1 small leek, chopped
2 onions, finely diced
2 large potatoes, peeled and
   diced quite small
1 garlic clove, crushed
2 litres (3½ pints/7 cups)
   vegetable stock, fresh or
   made from a stock cube
100 g (4 oz/½ cup) wild garlic
   (also known as ramsom),
   finely chopped
100 ml (3½ fl oz/½ cup)
   double cream
Salt and pepper

This may sound like quite an exotic soup,
but, it's really an old traditional British recipe.
It is very easy to make and the ingredients are
in abundance.

1 Thoroughly wash the nettle leaves, being careful not to
sting yourself (clean rubber gloves are probably the best
idea) and then place all of the ingredients except the wild
garlic and cream in a saucepan.

2 Bring to the boil and simmer for 40 minutes until the
potatoes are over soft. Add the wild garlic and cook for
1–2 minutes to heat through.

3 Pour the soup into a food processor or blender and blend
for 2 minutes. Season with salt and pepper.

4 Pour the blended soup back into the saucepan and bring
it back to the boil. The soup should be bright green in
appearance at this stage.

5 When you are ready to serve the soup stir through the
double cream and enjoy with fresh bread.

Note: Remember to use only the young, top leaves of the
nettle plant, as these are the most tender. Wild garlic is at
its most abundant between early spring and midsummer
and can be eaten raw or slightly cooked.

BE PREPARED For best results make at home before you go away. Transport to your
camp in a suitable container or flask and then reheat on site.

SEASIDE SOUP

From Peter Duncan (actor, TV presenter and former chief scout, 2004-2009)

SERVES 4

1 carrot, chopped

1 large onion, chopped

2 celery sticks, chopped (or
  1 head of fennel, sliced)

2 garlic cloves, chopped

200 g (7 oz) chopped seaweed
  (bladderwrack)

2 litres (3½ pints/8 cups)
  water

500 g (1 lb) fresh winkles and
  whelks (available from good
  fishmongers)

Salt and pepper

This recipe is easy to cook but hard to say! Scouting provides young people with the chance to realise their potential, to experience the freedom of the outdoors and to grow in independence and learn how to become true world citizens. They care for the world around them and for each other.

PETER DUNCAN

1 Place all the prepared vegetables in a large saucepan, including the bladderwrack. Cover with the water and season with a small amount of salt and pepper.

2 Put the saucepan over heat (fire, gas stove or barbecue grill) for about 1 hour – don't allow the liquid to boil.

3 After 1 hour, add the winkles and whelks (make sure they have been washed throughly).

4 Serve the broth with crusty French bread to mop up all the liquid.

TIP

If you're camping near the coast there can be plenty of 'free' food you can forage for, such as mussels, whelks, winkles and barnacles. Make sure the mussels are closed and the winkles and whelks have the little caps so you know they are still fresh.

WINTER MINESTRONE WARMER

SERVES 4-5

A drizzle of olive oil

I onion, finely chopped

I carrot, peeled and diced

I garlic clove, crushed

I celery stick, chopped

2 tablespoons tomato purée

2 litres (2 pints/7 cups)
   vegetable stock

I potato, peeled and diced

150 g (6 oz/½ cup) macaroni

I x 400 g tin black-eyed
   beans, drained and rinsed

I leek, finely diced

25 g (I oz/a little sprinkling)
   grated Parmesan cheese

Enjoy this comforting soup surrounded by friends and family looking into a roaring fire with a mug of soup accompanied by fresh bread – perfect for Bonfire Night. This is also best made the day before and heated up when you need it.

I Heat a little oil in a large saucepan. Add the onion, carrot, garlic and celery and cook for about 5–10 minutes until softened. Add the tomato purée and cook for 2–3 minutes.

2 Add the stock and potato and cook for 15 minutes. Add the macaroni and black-eyed beans and cook for 4–5 minutes.

3 Add the leek and leave to simmer for 10 minutes.

4 Finish with grated Parmesan cheese just before serving.

VARIATION
There are lots of other things you can add to minestrone soup such as freshly chopped tomatoes and freshly torn basil leaves.

 BE PREPARED This is perfect for making at home to be transported to camp in a suitable container or flask and reheated as needed.

PANCAKES

SERVES 4

125 g (4 oz/½ cup) self-
  raising flour
1 teaspoon baking powder
A pinch of salt
25 g (1 oz) caster sugar
200 ml (7 fl oz/⅔ cup)
  buttermilk
2 eggs
12 streaky bacon rashers
Vegetable oil, for frying
Maple syrup, to finish

Pancakes are far too good to be enjoyed only once a year on Shrove Tuesday. They are quick and easy to make and delicious when served with different toppings.

1 Sieve the flour, baking powder and salt into a large bowl and add the sugar. Whisk the buttermilk and eggs together in a separate bowl until smooth. Make a well in the centre of the flour and pour in the buttermilk mixture. Stir gently with a wooden spoon or spatula until just combined – don't overwork the mixture.

2 Fry the bacon in a little vegetable oil until crisp then drain and keep warm until needed.

3 Meanwhile, lightly oil a nonstick frying pan and spoon in 1–2 tablespoons of the batter per pancake. Small bubbles will start to appear in the batter. When the bubbles begin to burst the pancakes are ready to be flipped. Flip the pancakes and cook for a further minute. Serve immediately with maple syrup and the crispy bacon.

TOPPING IDEAS

Jam delights – cut some thick pancakes into squares. Spread a mixture of jam and peanut butter onto the squares and serve as a mid-morning or evening treat.

Lemon and sugar – top the pancakes with lemon juice and a sprinkling of caster sugar.

Banana and chocolate – top the pancakes with chocolate spread and sliced bananas.

Stewed fruits - top with your favourite stewed fruits (such as peaches, nectarines, blueberries or apples).

EGGS...

THE CAMPFIRE WAY

SERVES 1

1 large orange or potato

1 egg

YOU WILL ALSO NEED (OPTIONAL)

1 clean and empty tin (an old baked bean tin is ideal)

Some thin wire

1 night light or candle

The humble egg is one of the most versatile and nutritious of foods. Providing it survives the rough and tumble of camping, it can be cooked in the most unusual and delicious ways.

TO COOK AN EGG IN AN ORANGE

1 Cut the top third off the orange and carefully scoop out (and eat) the flesh, leaving just a peel shell. Break an egg into the orange shell and carefully place it in amongst the glowing campfire embers until you can see that the egg is cooked to your liking.

TO COOK AN EGG IN A POTATO

1 Wash the potato and cut the top off about one-third from the thinnest end (don't throw away the top). Scoop out the centre of the potato with a teaspoon, being careful not to pierce the side of it. It is important that you remove just the right amount of potato to accommodate the egg.

2 Break an egg and pour it into the cavity in the potato and replace the lid (the reserved potato top). Carefully wrap the potato in a double layer of foil and place it directly on the glowing campfire embers. Leave it to cook for about 30 minutes, turning it halfway through.

TO COOK AN EGG IN A TIN

1 Pierce a series of large holes in the side of the tin close to one end. Cut the bottom off to leave a cylinder. Tap a small hole in both ends of the egg with a needle. Thread a piece of wire through one hole and out the hole the other end.

2 Light the candle, place the tin over it and suspend the egg above it by threading the wire through the 2 holes in the tin. Cook for at least 5–10 minutes, turning occasionally.

SERVES 2
100 ml (3½ fl oz/⅓ cup) milk OR use a
mixture of milk and double cream
2 eggs
2 slices of bread
A knob of butter
Salt and pepper

EGGY BREAD

You can make this for breakfast on a Sunday morning whether at camp or at home. Serve the eggy bread with lashings of ketchup or with homemade jam for a change (just omit the salt and pepper).

- -

1 Mix the milk, cream (if using) and eggs in a bowl. Season with salt and pepper and give it another good whisk.

2 Dip the bread into the egg mix ensuring it is well coated and leave it to soak for 30 seconds. Meanwhile, heat the butter in a frying pan until it has melted.

3 Fry the soaked bread in the frying pan for 1–2 minutes per side.

NICK'S CORN ON THE COB

SERVES 4

4 fresh corn on the cob (½ or a whole one per person)
100 g (3½ oz/2 large knobs) salted butter
Chilli flakes, to taste
Salt and pepper

Freshly grilled corn on the cob, smeared with lots of butter, can be a sensational side dish. The difference between this and what you get out of a tin could not be greater.

1 Prepare the corn on the cobs by cutting the tops and bottoms off and removing the outer leaves.

2 Smear the cobs with butter and season with salt and pepper.

3 Lay the cobs out on a double layer of foil, sprinkle them with a little water, then wrap the foil into a parcel.

4 Place the foil parcel directly in the glowing campfire embers for about 15–20 minutes, turning occasionally.

5 Add even more butter and a small sprinkling of chilli flakes or garlic if liked after the cobs have cooked.

TRY SOMETHING DIFFERENT

• Bake in a prepared camp oven (see pages 22–5) – be aware that the timings may differ depending on the fire and how well your oven is made.

• Cook in a conventional oven preheated to 150°C (300°F), gas mark 2 for about 15 minutes.

CAMP PIZZAS

WITH CREATIVE TOPPINGS

SERVES 4

300 g (12 oz/1 and a bit cups)
   self-raising flour, plus
   extra for dusting
A pinch of salt
150 g (3 oz/⅔ cup) margarine
   or butter
250 ml (½ pint/1 cup) milk

A trip to a pizza restaurant is always fun, but why go to all the trouble if you can make delicious pizzas yourself.

1 Mix the flour, salt and margarine or butter with the milk to form a smooth, thick dough and knead on a lightly floured surface for 2–3 minutes.

2 Roll the dough out using a rolling pin or an empty wine bottle onto a double layer of foil that has been sprinkled with a little flour.

3 Place the foil onto the edge of hot campfire embers for about 15 minutes, then remove it to add your toppings.

4 Once you have topped your pizza (see suggestions below) return to the heat for a further 15 minutes. Check it frequently so that it doesn't burn.

TOPPING IDEAS

Classic Margarita – tomato pizza sauce, sliced mozzarella cheese, sun-dried tomatoes and basil leaves.

Breakfast pizza – tomato pizza sauce, bacon, sausage slices, mushrooms and a cracked egg on top.

Oriental surprise – cooked chicken, spring onions, cashew nuts and hoi sin or plum sauce.

Seafood platter – flaked cooked salmon, prawns, anchovies and Gruyère cheese.

TRY SOMETHING DIFFERENT

• Cook on a hot barbecue grill and add 10 minutes to the cooking time.

• Cook in an oven preheated to 160°C (325°F), gas mark 3 and reduce the total cooking time to 20 minutes.

SERVES 4
500 g (1 lb/4 cups) self-raising flour
75 g (3 oz/⅓ cup) caster sugar
200 ml (7 fl oz/⅔ cup) water
Chocolate spread or jam
You will also need a foil-covered stick

DAMPERS

The word classic does not do justice to this campfire treat.
Scouts have this recipe hardwired into their DNA.

1 Put your flour and sugar in a bowl and mix well. Gradually add the water a little at a time and knead gently until it forms a soft dough. Divide the dough into eight equal-sized pieces.

2 Roll each piece of dough in your hands until it is a long and thin sausage shape. Wrap it around a foil-covered stick and press to ensure it is well fixed in place.

3 Turning regularly, carefully hold the stick over an even heat (campfire or barbecue) for 10 minutes until hard to the touch.

4 Carefully slide the dampers off the stick and fill the cavity down the centre with chocolate spread or jam.

VARIATIONS Remove the sugar from the recipe and add a small amount of salt, maybe some grated Parmesan cheese or dried thyme for a savoury version.

FOR THE CARNIVORES AMONGST US, WE'RE SPOILED FOR CHOICE WHEN IT COMES TO OUTDOOR COOKING. FROM OLD FAVOURITES GIVEN A NEW TWIST, SUCH AS STUFFED SAUSAGES WITH QUICK ONION MARMALADE (SEE PAGE 72), TO GLOBAL FLAVOURS, SUCH AS LAMB TAGINE WITH LEMON AND CORIANDER COUSCOUS (SEE PAGE 93), YOUR ONLY DIFFICULTY WILL BE DECIDING WHICH TO TRY FIRST.

TOAD IN THE HOLE
WITH ONION GRAVY

SERVES 4

150 g (5 oz/⅔ cup) plain flour
I egg
230 ml (½ pint/I cup) milk
8 good-quality pork sausages
60 g (2 oz) margarine (or 6
    tablespoons vegetable oil)
Oil, for frying
I large onion, sliced
150 ml (¼ pint/½ cup) red
    wine (I large wine glass)
I beef stock cube
400 ml (14 fl oz/I½ cups)
    boiling water
Salt and pepper

TRY SOMETHING DIFFERENT

• This recipe would of
course work in a Dutch
oven - just keep an eye on
the batter to make sure it
doesn't burn on the bottom
of the pan - or for the
more adventurous a haybox
oven (see page 23)!

• You could alternatively
cook the sausages
separately in a frying
pan over the fire and
then make small savoury
pancakes with the same
batter and serve them
together - it works just
as well!

There's a myth that only mums know how to cook this properly. In fact there are few ingredients and it's very easy to make.

1 Preheat the oven to 150°C (300°F), gas mark 2 or prepare your chosen camp oven (see pages 22–5).

2 Mix the flour and egg together in a bowl and season with salt and pepper. Add the milk slowly while whisking until you have a smooth batter.

3 Place the sausages and margarine in a baking tray or ovenproof dish, and bake in the preheated or prepared oven for 15 minutes.

4 Take the pan or dish out of the oven and immediately pour your batter over the sausages – the batter should sizzle as it hits the hot margarine. Return the pan or dish to the oven for about 30–40 minutes or until the batter has risen and is golden in colour.

5 Meanwhile, make the onion gravy. Heat some oil in a frying pan, add the onion and cook until translucent. Pour over the red wine and bring to the boil. Crumble the stock cube into the wine and stir until thickened. Add boiling water to bring the gravy to your desired consistency.

6 Portion your toad in the hole and pour over lashings of gravy before serving. Personally, I think it is best served with mash!

SAUSAGE AND BEAN CASSOULET

SERVES 4

4 tablespoons olive oil
1 onion, sliced
1 garlic clove, crushed
8 sausages
150 g (6 oz) mini frankfurter
    sausages
2 tablespoons tomato purée
1 x 400 g tin chopped
    tomatoes
1 x 400 g tin cooked white
    beans
150 ml (¼ pint/⅔ cup)
    vegetable stock
1 tablespoon chopped basil
Salt and pepper

A real family favourite. Any variety of sausage can be used, but it's best with a Toulouse or try using wild boar.

1 Preheat the oven to 180°C (350°F), gas mark 4 or prepare a hay box oven (see page 23) or Dutch oven (see page 29).

2 Heat the oil in an ovenproof dish either over your campfire or on a camp stove. Add the onion and garlic and cook until softened.

3 Add the sausages to the dish and cook for 10–12 minutes until well browned. Remove the sausages, cut in half and return to the dish along with the frankfurter sausages.

4 Add the tomato purée, chopped tomatoes, beans and stock. Bring to the boil, season with salt and pepper and place in the preheated or prepared oven or over the glowing campfire embers for 30–40 minutes.

5 Stir through the basil just before serving.

VARIATIONS

· Why not add toasted pieces of French baguette to the top of the cassoulet just before serving.

· You can also use chickpeas as an alternative to beans.

BE PREPARED This recipe is ideal for making at home and bringing with you to be heated through over a campfire.

STUFFED SAUSAGES
WITH QUICK ONION MARMALADE

SERVES 2-4

8 sausages
150 g (5 oz/1½ cups) ricotta
   cheese
1 teaspoon wholegrain French
   mustard
2 tomatoes, sliced
Fresh baby gem or Cos
   lettuce leaves

FOR THE ONION MARMALADE

Butter or oil, for frying
4 red onions, thinly sliced
100 g (3½ oz/½ cup) caster
   sugar
1 thyme sprig
1 garlic clove, left whole
150 ml (¼ pint/½ cup) red
   wine (1 large wine glass)
Salt and pepper

Always treat the humble sausage with great respect. Make sure you get sausage with a high meat content and it's always worth asking locally to find the best varieties. Any flavour will work with this recipe – pork and apple is a winning combination.

1 Make the onion marmalade. Heat a little butter or oil in a frying pan and add the red onions. Cook until softened and then add the sugar, thyme, garlic and red wine. Remove the thyme sprig before serving.

2 Leave to gently simmer until the wine has nearly all gone and the onions are soft and almost spreadable (if the onions become too dry add a little water to avoid it catching on the bottom of the pan).

3 To prepare the sausages, grill the sausages on a hot barbecue, in a pan over glowing campfire embers or over a camp stove until cooked and then leave to cool.

4 Mix the ricotta cheese with the mustard in a bowl and season with salt and pepper.

5 Split the sausages down one side and fill each sausage with the ricotta mix and a little of the warm onion marmalade.

6 Serve with slices of fresh tomato and wrap in a lettuce leaf or a soft white bread roll.

SERVES UP TO 4

8–12 streaky or back bacon rashers
A drizzle of oil
100 g (4 oz/½ cup) mushrooms, sliced
4 small cooked potatoes, sliced (best if they
    are leftover from dinner!)
2 small tomatoes, cut in half and then
    sliced
4 large eggs

ALL-IN-ONE
COOKED BREAKFAST

Anything that saves washing up has got to be a
bonus, and this is a brilliant way to cook your
usual fry-up.

I Lay the bacon rashers in a large frying pan and drizzle
with a little oil. Cook the bacon until crispy and browned,
about 5–7 minutes, turning regularly.

2 Scatter over the mushrooms, slices of cooked potato and
tomato. Cook for a further 2–3 minutes.

3 Make space in the pan to crack the eggs in, leaving until
they are just set, or until the eggs are cooked to your liking.

VARIATION You can always mix all the ingredients
together once you've added the eggs to the pan, so they
scramble.

PORK 'N' PATTIES

SERVES 4

4 pork chops
50 g (2 oz/a large knob)
   butter or margarine
1 apple, cored and sliced
100 ml (¼ pint/½ cup) apple
   juice
200 g (8 oz/1 cup) stale
   breadcrumbs
200 g (8 oz/1 cup) grated
   cheese (I love this recipe
   with Cornish Yarg!)
2 onions, finely chopped
25 g (1 oz/a good-sized pinch)
   dried mixed herbs
2 eggs, beaten
Salt and pepper

TRY SOMETHING DIFFERENT

• Bake the foil parcels
in a prepared camp oven
(see pages 22-5), Dutch
oven (see page 29)
or on a hot barbecue
grill for the same
amount of time.

Pork and apple are a classic combination, but I bet you've never tried this.

- -

1 Make a double layer of foil for each chop large enough to wrap around the meat. Top each chop with some butter, a couple of apple slices and a little of the apple juice and seal the foil so that you have 4 individual flat parcels.

2 Place the foil parcel directly on the edge of the glowing campfire embers for about 20 minutes per side (taking care when turning the parcel).

3 To make the patties, mix the breadcrumbs, cheese, onions and the mixed herbs with the beaten egg and a little of the apple juice in a bowl. Season to taste.

4 Shape the mixture into small patties about 1 cm (½ inch) thick and lay them out on a double layer of foil.

5 Carefully place the foil on the edge of the glowing campfire embers for about 10 minutes on each side (taking care when turning the patties).

6 Serve the chops with the patties and a choice of vegetables and potatoes.

HIGHLAND FILLER

From Paul Liversidge (youth leader)

SERVES 4

125 g (4 oz) small new
   potatoes
Oil, for frying
4 chicken breasts, cut into
   chunks
2 onions, finely chopped
2 peppers, any colour,
   deseeded and chopped
125 g (4 oz) mushrooms,
   chopped (optional)
1 x 500 g jar pasta sauce
Crusty bread, rice or pasta,
   to serve

This is an all-in-one-pan recipe. The best meat to use is chicken, depending on how many people you're cooking for. It's great for a cold night while on camp especially if everyone likes comfort food. It's an inexpensive and filling meal for an evening sitting round the campfire feeling warm inside.

1 Bring a saucepan of water to the boil and par-boil the potatoes for about 10 minutes. Drain the potatoes and leave to cool.

2 Heat a little oil in a frying pan set over a medium heat. Add the chicken to the hot pan and fry for a few minutes until sealed all over.

3 Add the onions to the pan and cook slowly until the chicken starts to brown and the onions begin to soften and turn translucent, about 5–8 minutes. Add the peppers and mushrooms and cook until soft, about 3–5 minutes. Pour in the pasta sauce.

4 Slice the par-boiled potatoes and add them to the pan, bring to the boil and cook for 5–10 minutes to make sure everything is piping hot.

5 Serve either on its own or with crusty bread, rice or pasta.

TIP

This is also ideal for vegetarians – just remove the chicken and add whatever other vegetables you like.

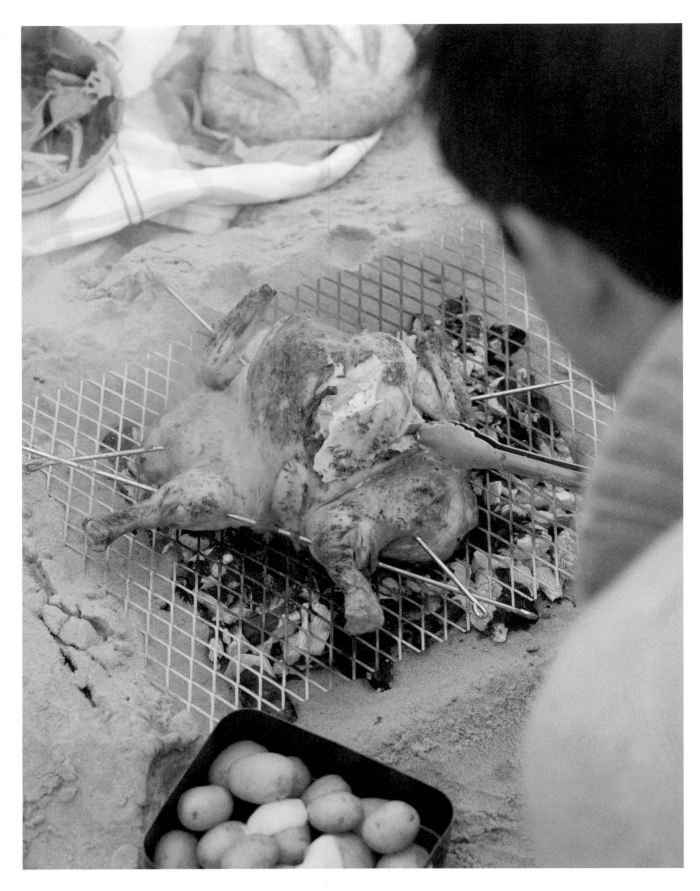

SPATCHCOCK CHICKEN
WITH LEMON, GARLIC AND THYME

SERVES 4-6

1 whole chicken, weighing about 1.5–1.8 kg (3–3½ lb), spatchcocked (get your butcher to do this for you)

100 g (4 oz/a large knob) butter

2 lemons, zested and juiced (keep the remaining squeezed lemons)

Half a bunch of fresh thyme, about 50 g (2 oz)

Salt and pepper

Cooked new potatoes, to serve

Here is another delicious recipe for your outdoor dining room.

1 Wash the whole chicken and pat dry. Use metal skewers to pierce the leg of the chicken and push through diagonally so that it comes out through the wing on the other side. Push another skewer through the other leg going the other way diagonally, so the skewers are crossed.

2 Mix the butter, lemon juice, zest and thyme together in a bowl. Season well and mix until the butter is spreadable. Gently pull back the skin on the breast of the chicken and use your fingers to spread the butter under the skin. Pull the skin back over the chicken, ensuring it is sitting tightly and not flapping loose.

3 Sprinkle the skin of the chicken with any leftover thyme and spread any butter that is left over.

4 Place the skewered chicken onto a grid set over glowing campfire embers.

5 Turn the chicken regularly and after about 15–20 minutes, when the skin is golden brown and crispy, remove the skewers and wrap the chicken in a double layer of foil.

6 Place the foil parcel directly on the embers and leave it to cook for a further 45 minutes, turning every 20 minutes or so. Check the chicken in the centre of the breast and legs to check if they are well cooked (the juices will run clear from the centre if the bird is cooked). Serve with freshly cooked new potatoes.

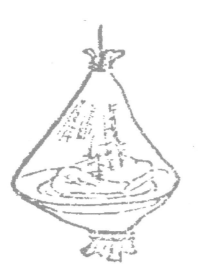

SERVES 4

Oil, for frying

4 chicken breasts, cut into thin strips

2 onions, sliced

3 green or red peppers, deseeded and cut
   into strips

2 teaspoons (a good pinch) ground cumin

2 teaspoons (a good pinch) smoked paprika

Juice of 1 lime

8 soft flour tortillas or Moroccan
   Flatbreads (see page 44)

Salt

SUMMER CAMP FAJITAS

This is perfect for any summer camp. It's a great sharing
dish and can be made for any number of people – the more
the merrier. And very little washing up, too.

1 Heat some oil in a frying pan and fry the strips of chicken for about
10 minutes. Remove from the pan and set aside.

2 Add the onions and peppers together with the spices to the pan, and
fry for about 10 minutes, until softened.

3 Return the chicken to the pan, pour over the lime juice and season
with a little salt.

4 Using the tortillas or flatbreads as a plate, pile some of the chicken
mix onto it, roll up and enjoy.

TIP

This is also great if you add soured cream, fresh guacamole or a
homemade tomato salsa when you roll the tortillas up.

PITTED CHICKEN

SERVES 4-6

½ loaf of stale bread
1 carrot, grated
1 onion, grated
2 celery sticks, grated
150 ml (¼ pint/⅔ cup) milk
1 egg
40 g (1½ oz) fresh sage leaves
   or 25 g (1 oz/a good pinch)
   dried
1 whole chicken, weighing
   about 1.5–1.8 kg (3–3½ lb)
A knob of butter or
   margarine
Salt and pepper
Foil-roasted Squash and
   Aubergine (see page 136),
   to serve

This needs a little forward planning, but once it's started cooking you can leave it and enjoy your day in the great outdoors.

1 Prepare your pit fire (see below).

2 Break the bread into small pieces (try using a grater) and mix it with the carrot, onion and celery in a bowl. Add the milk, egg, sage and plenty of salt and pepper and mix together well.

3 Prepare the chicken (remember to store your chicken in a cool box or fridge until you're ready to cook) and stuff the bread mix into the cavity and under the skin of the bird. Remember to pull the skin back to cover the stuffing, then rub the outside of the bird with butter and seasoning. Wrap the whole bird in three layers of foil and place in the prepared pit fire. The chicken simply lies on top of the embers and the earth is piled on top of it.

4 Leave the chicken to cook for about 3 hours. Check the chicken in the centre of the breast and legs to check if they are cooked (the juices will run clear from the centre if the bird is cooked). Serve with vegetables, which can be wrapped in a separate foil parcel and cooked alongside the chicken in the last 30–40 minutes. Serve with the roasted squash and aubergine.

MAKING A PIT FIRE

Dig a hole in the ground 30 cm (12 inches) square. Build and light a fire (see page 25) in the pit and let it burn for 45 minutes to give good-quality glowing embers before cooking on it. Place your well-wrapped food on top of the embers and then top with earth so that it is completely covered.

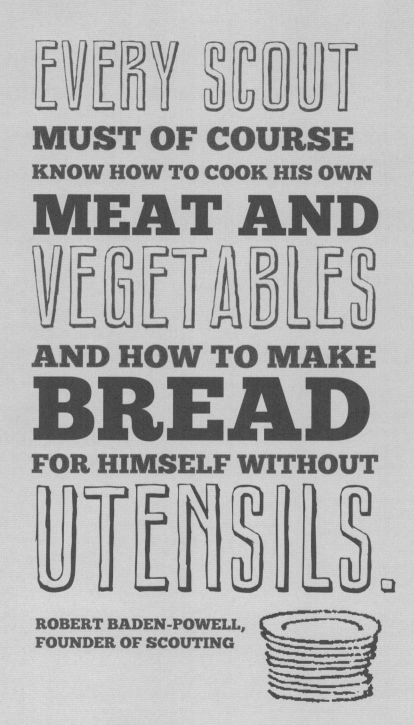

EVERY SCOUT
MUST OF COURSE
KNOW HOW TO COOK HIS OWN
MEAT AND
VEGETABLES
AND HOW TO MAKE
BREAD
FOR HIMSELF WITHOUT
UTENSILS.

**ROBERT BADEN-POWELL,
FOUNDER OF SCOUTING**

THAI GREEN CURRY
WITH LEMONGRASS JASMINE RICE

SERVES 4

1 tablespoon (a good drizzle) vegetable oil

500 g (1 lb/2 cups) diced chicken breast

300 g (12 oz/1¼ cups) diced aubergine

200 g (8 oz/1 cup) baby corn

1 x 400 ml tin coconut milk

400 g (1 lb/2 cups) jasmine rice

2 lemongrass stalks, bruised

2–3 kaffir lime leaves

400 ml (¾ pint/2 cups) water

40 g (1½ oz) chopped coriander

FOR THE CURRY PASTE

1 lemongrass stalk

1–3 green chillies

1 shallot, finely chopped

2 garlic cloves

A 2.5-cm (1-inch) piece of peeled fresh ginger

50 g (2 oz/½ bunch) fresh coriander

½ teaspoon ground cumin

2 tablespoons sugar

3–4 tablespoons coconut milk

Salt and pepper

You can of course make this without the chicken to create a great vegetarian dish.

- -

1 Firstly, make the curry paste. Put the lemongrass, chilli, shallot, garlic, ginger, coriander, cumin and sugar in a food processor or blender or a pestle and mortar. Blend or grind into a paste using a little coconut milk to bind the ingredients together. Season to taste.

2 Heat the oil in a frying pan, add the chicken and fry for about 10 minutes, until browned. Add the curry paste and cook for about 2 minutes.

3 Add the diced aubergine, baby sweetcorn and the coconut milk and leave to simmer for 30–40 minutes.

4 Meanwhile, put the rice, lemongrass, lime leaves and water in another saucepan and bring to the boil. Cook the rice for about 10 minutes, or until light and fluffy. Drain the rice, serve with lashings of curry and top with chopped coriander.

TIP

If you can't get hold of kaffir lime leaves, half a lime added to the rice during cooking will work just as well.

 BE PREPARED It may look like a lot of ingredients but the curry paste can be made up to 1 week in advance, refrigerated and then taken on camp with you.

HAWAIIAN CHICKEN

WITH COCONUT AND PINEAPPLE

SERVES 4

4 chicken breasts, skinless and boneless

1 x 150 g tin pineapple chunks in natural juice

100 g (4 oz/about ½ cup) cashew nuts

1 x 400 g tin coconut milk

400 g (13 oz/2 cups) basmati rice

Salt and pepper

Here is another dish to bring sunshine to your summer even if the weather is looking cloudy.

1 Clean and prepare the chicken breasts and place them on a double layer of foil or in a foil bag.

2 Season the chicken, pour over a little of the juice from the tin of pineapple, scatter over the cashew nuts and add half of the coconut milk. Seal the parcel or bag.

3 In a separate foil parcel or bag add the rice, pineapple chunks and the remaining coconut milk. Seal the foil parcel or bag.

4 Place the chicken parcel directly onto hot campfire embers and leave to cook for at least 40 minutes, carefully turning the parcels frequently.

5 Add the rice parcels to the embers after 30 minutes.

6 Serve the chicken with the rice and enjoy.

TIP

Try not to buy your chicken too far in advance, and always store it in a cool box until you're ready to cook it.

EVEREST STEW

from Bear Grylls

SERVES 6-8

8 chicken-breast-size hunks
   of meat from the leg of
   a yak (you might prefer
   lamb)

Yak lard, for frying (you can
   use olive oil)

4 onions, chopped

6 carrots, chopped

Garlic (if you have it), finely
   chopped

Any herbs you can find
   growing nearby

A slug of red wine (or any
   local liquor)

5 generous handfuls of brown
   rice

Coarse sea salt

On the British Everest expedition I was part of
some years back, we became all too familiar with
this sort of stew-cum-risotto. It was a dish we
ate almost solidly for three months. One yak makes
90 stews, and of course first up they had to be
slaughtered, but at least no freezer was needed
– it was –20°C outside, so you'd just leave a leg
outside the tent and it would freeze. It wasn't a
bad dish actually – a bit sinewy at times, but for
the experience you can recreate this with any meat
that's a little gamey. I once added nettles which
were pretty good, but sadly you don't get many of
them growing around the Everest base-camp.

BEAR GRYLLS

1 Make an open fire and grab your cooking pot.

2 Chop the meat into chunks and fry them in the lard or
oil. Next add the onions, carrots and garlic and fry for
a little longer. Add some salt, the herbs and the wine.
(Actually, we only had a bottle of whisky, for medicinal
purposes, but that had to do.)

3 Finally add the rice and an ample amount of snow on
top of it all to provide the water. Leave it to cook for as
long as you like until it looks like a risotto-ish stew. Repeat
for 3 months, then climb Everest.

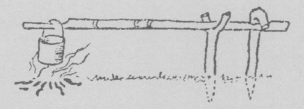

SPICY LAMB, TOMATO AND COCONUT CURRY

From Anjum Anand

SERVES 4

1 tablespoon coriander seeds
1 teaspoon cumin seeds
15 black peppercorns
A 5-cm (2-inch) cinnamon
    stick
4 cloves
500 g (1 lb) boneless lamb leg
    or shoulder, cubed (or 600
    g (1 lb 3 oz) bone in)
3 small onions, finely
    chopped
3 tomatoes, chopped
15 g (½ oz) peeled ginger,
    grated into a paste
8 fat garlic cloves, grated into
    a paste
3–6 green chillies, whole but
    pierced
500 ml (17 fl oz/2 cups) water
2 tablespoons ghee (or half
    vegetable oil and butter)
200–300 ml (7–10 fl oz/
    about 1 cup) coconut milk,
    or to taste
1½ teaspoons lemon juice, or
    to taste
Salt
Indian breads, to serve

I have missed out on Scouting so far and am now
waiting for my children to get old enough to take
them so I can finally experience it!

ANJUM ANAND

– –

1 Using a spice grinder, mortar and pestle or the end of a
clean rolling pin, pound the whole spices to a fine powder.

2 Place the lamb, two of the onions, tomatoes, ginger,
garlic, chillies, freshly ground spices and salt in a large
saucepan. Add the water, bring to the boil, cover and cook
gently for 45–60 minutes, or until the lamb is cooked and
tender. Give the pot a stir every 10 minutes or so.

3 After about 45 minutes, melt the ghee in a small
saucepan and fry the remaining onion until well browned.

4 There shouldn't be too much liquid left in the pan once
the lamb is cooked, but if necessary, cook off any excess
moisture over a high flame for 6–7 minutes, stirring
quite often, until the sauce has mostly been absorbed by
the lamb. This 'bhunoing' or browning process will help
homogenise the sauce and deepen the flavours. Add the
browned onion and ghee.

5 Pour in the coconut milk and lemon juice, bring to a boil
and simmer for 5 minutes; the sauce should be thick and
creamy. Taste and adjust the seasoning, adding lemon juice
or coconut milk until the dish is perfect for you, then serve
with Indian breads.

TIP
If you don't have ghee, then use half oil and half butter.

ROAST LEG OF LAMB

SERVES 6

1.5–2 kg (3–4 lb) leg of lamb,
  de-boned and rolled (ask
  your butcher to do this)
A selection of vegetables of
  your choice — my favourite
  with lamb is young
  tenderstem broccoli, baby
  carrots and sautéed leeks
Minted new potatoes, to serve

There's no reason why Sunday lunch cooked outdoors can't be every bit as refined, tasty and sociable as when it is cooked in your kitchen at home. The only difference is that your dinner party music is birdsong and your table and chairs are tree stumps.

---

1 Skewer the lamb through the middle lengthways using wire or a thin metal skewer – this ensures the lamb can be turned easily while it is cooking over the fire.

2 Place the skewered lamb on 2 forked sticks, preferably one taller than the other, so the lamb is at a slight angle – this will allow the cooking juices and fat to be collected in a tin or metal mug rather than dripping onto the embers.

3 Cook the lamb over a large amount of glowing embers for about 1½ hours, turning frequently. Use the collected juices to baste the meat during the cooking time.

4 Serve with a selection of vegetables of your choice and minted new potatoes.

TIPS

· Try not to buy your roasting joint too far in advance, and store it in a cool box while you prepare the fire.

· Peel and chop your vegetables before getting your lamb on to cook. This way you won't be distracted from turning your lamb and will reduce the risk of burning it.

· You will need a large amount of glowing embers to keep this roast cooking for the right amount of time.

TRY SOMETHING DIFFERENT

· To cook on a hot barbecue, split the saddle down the middle to make a thinner piece for easier cooking. It is best to use a barbecue with a lid to create an oven-like atmosphere. Cook for about 30-40 minutes depending on how you like it cooked.

· This method also works with joints of beef, such as topside or even sirloin.

LAMB TAGINE

WITH LEMON AND CORIANDER COUSCOUS

SERVES 4

½ tablespoon ground
   cinnamon
½ tablespoon ground cumin
½ tablespoon ground
   turmeric
Olive oil, for frying
600 g (1 lb 3 oz) diced lamb
   (shoulder or neck are best)
2 onions, finely chopped
1 garlic clove
1 tablespoon tomato purée
1 x 400 g tin chopped
   tomatoes
250 ml (8 fl oz/1 cup)
   chicken stock
75 g (3 oz/a small handful)
   dried apricots
1 x 400 g tin chickpeas,
   drained and rinsed
Salt and pepper

FOR THE COUSCOUS

250 g (8 oz/1 cup) couscous
Olive oil
Juice and zest of 1 lemon
350 ml (12 fl oz/1½ cups)
   hot fresh chicken stock (or
   made from a stock cube)
A handful of finely chopped
   coriander

This is a great alternative to your usual camping stew, adding a bit of the exotic to your outdoor meal. You can also make it in advance at home, then reheat it when you get to your campsite.

1 Mix half of the ground spices together in a small bowl and add a little oil to make into a paste. Rub this paste into the diced lamb so that it is well covered and leave to marinate overnight in a cool place, preferably a fridge or cool box.

2 Thread the lamb onto 3–4 metal skewers and cook it over the glowing campfire embers for about 10–15 minutes.

3 Heat some oil in a frying pan and fry the onions for about 5–10 minutes, until softened. Add the garlic and remaining spices. Cook for about 1 minute. Add the tomato purée, chopped tomatoes and chicken stock, season with salt and pepper and simmer for 20–30 minutes.

4 Add the dried apricots and chickpeas to the simmering tomato mixture and leave it to simmer for 10 minutes. If you find the tagine is quite dry, you can add more stock or water if necessary.

5 Meanwhile, make the couscous. Coat the couscous with olive oil, lemon juice and zest and season well. Pour over the hot stock, cover with cling film and leave for 10 minutes. Fluff the couscous with a fork and add the chopped coriander before serving with the tagine and lamb.

TIP

For this dish you could cut the pieces of lamb smaller to speed up the cooking process, or add less liquid.

MINCED KEBABS

SERVES 6

2 eggs

250 g (8 oz/1 cup) oatmeal or
  breadcrumbs

500 g (1 lb) minced lamb

2 red onions, cut into
  2.5-cm (1-inch) cubes

1 green pepper, cut into
  2.5-cm (1-inch) cubes

12 cherry tomatoes

Salt and pepper

These kebabs are a great way of breaking out of the 'sausages and burgers' mentality when it comes to barbecues and outdoor cooking.

- -

1 Beat the eggs well in a mixing bowl and then add the oatmeal or breadcrumbs. Add the minced lamb, and using clean hands, mix well until a thick dough forms. Season well with salt and pepper. Roll the mix into balls about 2.5 cm (1 inch) in diameter. Transfer the rolled balls to the fridge for 30 minutes to set. If you're on camp, place them in the cool box or find the best possible refrigeration available.

2 Make 6 skewers from a green stick by removing the bark and sealing it by holding it briefly over the glowing campfire embers. Alteratively, use metal skewers. Onto these thread the rolled meatballs, red onions and peppers in an alternate pattern.

3 Position a grill above the glowing embers of your campfire, place the kebabs on top and cook for about 15 minutes, turning them only once or twice to avoid the meat breaking up.

HOW TO MAKE A GREEN STICK

Green stick skewers are a brilliant camp cooking tool and are perfect for this recipe and any others involving skewering food. Perfect types of wood for using as a green stick skewer are oak, birch and apple. Remember the piece of wood must be alive and green, with the bark stripped off and one end sharpened to a point if required.

4 After this time, thread the cherry tomatoes onto the end of each skewer and put them back over the heat for a further 5 minutes.

5 Serve these along with the Tangy Kebabs (see page 96) for a colourful, delicious outdoor meal.

TANGY KEBABS

SERVES 6

1 kg (2 lb) diced leg of lamb, cut into 2.5-cm (1-inch) cubes

2 red peppers, cut into 2.5-cm (1-inch) cubes

12 small round button mushrooms

12 small round shallots, peeled

FOR THE MARINADE

4 tablespoons dark soy sauce

4 tablespoons sesame oil

2 tablespoons sweet chilli sauce

2 tablespoons rice vinegar or white wine vinegar

2 tablespoons tomato sauce

25 g (1 oz) finely chopped coriander

Sample a taste of the Orient with these sweet and spicy kebabs (see page 95 for photograph).

1 Firstly mix all of the marinade ingredients together in a mixing bowl.

2 Add the diced lamb, cover the bowl and transfer to the fridge or a cool box to marinate for at least 2 hours.

3 Once marinated, prepare your skewers – preferably metal or green sticks (see page 94) with the bark removed. Thread the marinated lamb onto the skewer and alternate with the diced peppers, mushrooms and shallots.

4 Place the kebabs over hot campfire embers or on a hot barbecue grill for about 20 minutes. Any of the liquid marinade that is left can be basted over the kebabs during the cooking process.

TRY SOMETHING DIFFERENT

• Try using diced beef, chicken and turkey.

• You can replace some of the vegetables with other varieties such as courgettes or butternut squash.

BE PREPARED Marinate the meat at home and then take it with you in a suitable container ready to cook.

ONE MAN STEW

SERVES 1

1 carrot
1 onion
1 potato
Oil or butter, for frying
150 g (6 oz/⅔ cup) diced beef
100 ml (3½ fl oz/a medium-sized wine glass) red wine
1 garlic clove
25 g (1 oz/about half a bunch) thyme
1 beef stock cube
600 ml (1 pint/1½ cups) water
Salt and pepper

Don't panic, this doesn't have to be made for only one person (or a man for that matter) – just multiply the ingredients for the number of people you're cooking for. It's a proper winter warmer.

1 Peel and prepare the vegetables and cut them all into 2.5-cm (1-inch) cubes – they need to be quite chunky to withstand the long cooking process.

2 Heat a little oil or butter in an oven- or fireproof dish, add the beef and fry for 10 minutes, until the meat has browned. Use a slotted spoon to remove the beef from the dish and set aside.

3 Add the carrots and onions to the same pan you browned the beef in and fry for 5–8 minutes, until softened, making sure you scrape all the sticky bits of beef from the bottom of the pan.

4 Pour in the wine, add the garlic and thyme and crumble the stock cube into the pan. Add the water and then return the beef to the pan.

5 Cover with a lid and allow to simmer for about 30 minutes. You can then either leave the dish on the campfire embers or put it on a camp stove to simmer for a further 1½ hours.

6 Add the potatoes when you have about 40 minutes of cooking time left.

BE PREPARED Prepare and cook the stew at home and transport it to camp in a suitable container ready to be reheated when needed.

BURGER TWISTS

SERVES 4-6

FOR THE DOUGH

500 g (1 lb/2 cups) plain
    flour
60 g (2¼ oz/¼ cup) butter or
    margarine
A pinch of salt
50 ml (2 fl oz/4–5
    tablespoons) water

FOR THE BURGER MIX

1 egg, beaten
500 g (1 lb/2 cups) minced
    beef or chicken
½ onion, grated
25 g (1 oz/¼ cup)
    breadcrumbs
Salt and pepper

This is a true Scouting recipe. The twist is
something that every young person knows how to
cook on a fire. Here's a way of turning it into a
complete meal.

- -

1 First, make the dough. Mix the flour, butter or margarine
and salt together with the water to make a thick dough.

2 Turn the dough out onto a lightly floured surface and
stretch it into a long sausage shape. Start to wrap it around
a sturdy green stick (see page 94) in a traditional 'twist'
style, leaving gaps of 1 cm (½ inch) as you go up the stick.
Repeat with 7 more green sticks.

3 Now, make the burger mix. Mix the egg, minced beef
or chicken, grated onion and breadcrumbs together in a
mixing bowl and season well.

4 Roll the mix into a sausage shape and coil this around the
stick, filling in between the rolls of dough.

5 Either wrap the whole thing in some foil that has been
lightly greased with vegetable oil and cook in the glowing
campfire embers or support the sticks over the embers
on two forked sticks for about 15–20 minutes, turning
regularly until cooked.

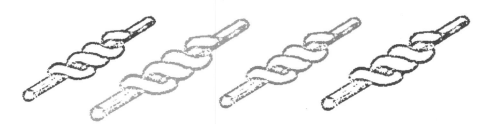

BEEF AND FENNEL KOFTAS

From James Martin

SERVES 4

500 g (1 lb/2 cups) minced
  beef
1 garlic clove, peeled
½ teaspoon ground fennel
3–4 tablespoons olive oil
75 g (3 oz) mixed salad leaves
  of your choice
Juice of ½ lemon
1 tablespoon extra-virgin
  olive oil
Salt and pepper
1 lemon, cut into wedges, to
  serve
4 corn on the cob, to serve

My memories of Scouting are wood smoke, laughing with friends and hot food at the end of a tiring day. The food may have got more sophisticated, but these are still among my favourite things. Have a go at this fun outdoor dish and make sure you get your friends around!

JAMES MARTIN

1 Soak 8 small wooden skewers for 10 minutes in cold water.

2 Place the beef in a bowl, grate in the garlic and add the ground fennel. Season with salt and pepper, mix and divide the mixture into 8 pieces.

3 Having first dipped your hands in cold water to stop the meat sticking to them, thread each section of mince onto a soaked wooden skewer. Press into shape around the skewer and place in the fridge or a cool box for 1 hour to firm up.

4 Set a griddle pan or frying pan over a high heat, brush each kofta with a little of the olive oil and place in the pan to cook for about 2–3 minutes on each side.

5 Place the salad leaves in a bowl and dress with the lemon juice and the extra-virgin olive oil. Season with salt and pepper and mix gently.

6 Remove the koftas from the pan and serve 2 per person. Serve with the mixed salad, a wedge of lemon and grilled sweetcorn straight from the barbecue or campfire embers.

BE PREPARED Make the kebabs at home and then transport them to camp for a handy ready to cook camp dinner.

COWBOY DINNER

SERVES 4

300 g (10 oz/1 ½ cups)
  minced beef or lamb
½ tablespoon chilli powder
1 x 200 g tin red kidney
  beans, rinsed and drained
12 streaky bacon rashers
4 potatoes, peeled and sliced
2 small onions, sliced
Salt and pepper

TRY SOMETHING DIFFERENT

• Cook on a hot barbecue
or in a conventional
oven preheated to 150°C
(300°F), gas mark 2 for
the same amount of time.

This is a great recipe to try if your cooking space is limited, as it all gets cooked together.

1 Mix together the minced beef or lamb, chilli powder, kidney beans and seasoning in a mixing bowl.

2 Lay out a double layer of foil about 20 cm (8 inches) square. Lay 3 rashers of bacon in the centre about 2.5 cm (1 inch) apart.

3 Place a few slices of potato on top of the bacon, then top with one-quarter of the beef mix, then some of the sliced onions and then finish with a few more potato slices.

4 Wrap the edges of the bacon around the top of the potato to form a parcel and then fold the whole thing in the foil to make a parcel. Duplicate this parcel for each diner, so everyone's got their own.

5 Put the foil parcels directly at the edge of the glowing campfire embers and cook for about 30 minutes, turning frequently to ensure even cooking. Unwrap and enjoy.

SOME PEOPLE **PREFER MEAT TO FISH** BECAUSE THEY'RE WORRIED THEY'LL LEAVE THE TABLE HUNGRY. REALLY, THEY'RE MISSING OUT ON A WHOLE WORLD OF **BRILLIANT TEXTURES AND FLAVOURS.** FISH AVAILABLE AROUND THE WORLD IS **FRESH AND DELICIOUS** AND IT'S EVEN BETTER WHEN **YOU CATCH IT YOURSELF.** YOU WON'T GET ANY COMPLAINTS WITH THIS COLLECTION OF RECIPES.

TEA-SMOKED MACKEREL

SERVES 4

4 medium mackerel,
 weighing about 300–400 g
 (10–13 oz) each
8 teabags (English breakfast
 preferably)
A small handful of rice
 (any variety)
25 g (1 oz/a large sprinkling)
 caster sugar
A knob of butter or
 margarine
Salt and pepper
Fresh bread and salad,
 to serve

TRY SOMETHING DIFFERENT

• Why not try smoking
with different flavours
of teabags.

• Try putting fresh herbs
like rosemary, sage or
even lavender straight
into the campfire
embers to create some
wonderfully aromatic
smoke.

• Cook the foil parcels
on a hot barbecue for the
same amount of time.

What could be simpler than a good fish well cooked? This recipe is a novel way of getting the subtle flavour of tea infused into fresh mackerel.

1 Prepare the fish by removing the innards and cleaning the inside thoroughly. Make 3–4 diagonal slits into the skin of each fish using a sharp knife, making sure not to go too deep into the flesh.

2 Lay out a double layer of foil and sprinkle the contents of 2 opened teabags, some of the rice and caster sugar in the centre. Cover this with a single sheet of foil.

3 Place 1 mackerel on top of the single sheet of foil, spread a knob of butter or margarine onto the skin of the fish, season well and wrap the foil loosely round to create a parcel. Make sure there is space for the smoke to circulate within the foil parcel. Make 3 more parcels in the same way using the remaining mackerels and ingredients.

4 Place the foil parcels directly on the glowing campfire embers and leave to smoke for about 10 minutes. The flesh of the fish should flake away from the skin with ease when it is cooked.

5 This is perfect served with fresh bread and salad.

TIP
Gut and de-head the mackerel before anything else or get a fishmonger to do this for you.

FISH IN NEWSPAPER

STUFFED WITH LEMON AND FENNEL

SERVES 4

4 whole fish (such as
   mackerel, trout or small
   sea bass), weighing about
   300–400 g (10–13 oz) each
2 lemons, sliced
2 whole fennel bulbs, sliced
25 g (1 oz/about ½ a bunch)
   fresh dill
Salt and pepper

YOU WILL ALSO NEED

Plenty of newspaper

TRY SOMETHING DIFFERENT

• Cook the paper
parcel on top of a hot
barbecue grill for the
same amount of time.

• Try different stuffing
combinations, such as
thyme and garlic or
basil with pine nuts
and tomato.

This is a classic outdoor dish – a fish cooked with the minimum of fuss. Whether you've caught it yourself or you've cheated, this is about unlocking the great flavours of your fish. The newspaper adds a wonderful smoky flavour.

1 Prepare the fish by removing the innards and cleaning the inside thoroughly. Soak 5–6 sheets of newspaper in a bowl of cold water.

2 Stuff the inside of each fish with slices of lemon, fennel and some dill. Season well with salt and pepper.

3 Lay out 4–5 sheets of the soaked newspaper and place one of the stuffed fish in the centre. Wrap the paper around the fish tightly (the paper will stay closed by itself because it is wet). Use the remaining fish and soaked newspaper to make 3 more parcels.

4 Place the paper parcels directly onto the glowing campfire embers for about 10 minutes, turning once or twice and making sure the newspaper does not burn too much. Unwrap and enjoy, taking care over the tiny bones when eating the fish.

TIP

Remember to hang on to your newspapers. Tabloid is better than broadsheet for the quality of the paper rather than the news coverage!

STEAMED SEA BASS
WITH PRAWNS

SERVES 4

2 whole sea bass, weighing
about 300–500 g
(10 oz–1 lb) each
8–12 large raw prawns,
de-headed but unpeeled
1 lemon
Roasted Potato Wedges
(see page 48) and herby
mayonnaise, to serve

YOU WILL ALSO NEED

A good armful of long wild
grass

This looks really impressive on an open fire;
even more so if you try it at home on a barbecue.
Remember to ask the fishmonger for your fish to
be gutted and scaled.

1 Make 2–3 diagonal slits into the skin of each fish using a
sharp knife, making sure not to go too deep into the flesh.

2 Carefully wet the long grass and spread half of it evenly
either over a barbecue grill or straight onto the glowing
campfire embers.

3 Lay the fish and prawns on top of the grass then spread
the remaining grass on top of the fish so that it is well
covered. The grass will hiss and steam. You can keep
flicking it with water to prevent it from burning.

4 The fish will take about 10 minutes each side, depending
on their size. The prawns will be done when they have
changed from a blue/grey to a bright pink colour.

5 Carefully remove the shell from the prawns and skin
from the fish. Cut the lemon into wedges and serve with
the fish and prawns, Roasted Potato Wedges and herby
mayonnaise.

VARIATION

Try adding some herbs to the fish before you steam – wild
sorrel or dill would work well with sea bass.

CAMP CURED TROUT
WITH MUSTARD AND DILL CRUST

SERVES 3-4

2 large fresh rainbow trout
   fillets, de-scaled and pin
   boned, weighing about
   125 g (4 oz) each
250 g (8 oz/1 cup) fine table
   salt
250 g (8 oz/1 cup) caster
   sugar
100 g (3½ oz/1 big bunch)
   dill, leaves finely chopped
   and stalks reserved for the
   marinade
20 whole peppercorns
40 g (1½ oz/2 tablespoons)
   wholegrain mustard
Fresh bread and lemon juice,
   to serve

You could use salmon rather than the trout if you
are catering for larger numbers.

- -

1 Firstly wash the trout fillets and pat dry. Make 2 slits into
the skin side of the fillets using a sharp knife, making sure
not to go too deep into the flesh.

2 Mix the salt, sugar, dill stalks and peppercorns together
in a bowl. Sprinkle a layer of the curing mix onto the
bottom of a dish large enough to fit the trout fillets next to
each other.

3 Lay the trout fillets skin side down and then sprinkle the
remaining curing mix over the top of the fish. Wrap the
dish with cling film and refrigerate (find the best possible
way of refrigeration – a cool box or a fridge on the campsite
if you are not preparing at home) for at least 24 hours and
no longer than 48 hours.

4 Once the curing process has finished, the flesh of the fish
should feel firm to the touch and become darker in colour.
Wash any excess salt and sugar off the fillets and pat dry
again: they should feel quite rigid.

5 Spread the wholegrain mustard over the flesh of the trout
and then sprinkle generously with the finely chopped dill.

6 Using a long sharp knife, slice the trout at a slight angle,
so you get a bit of the crust with every slice. Enjoy with
fresh bread and a little lemon juice.

BE PREPARED This recipe can be made 2–3 days in advance. So it could be made at
home, wrapped well in cling film or an airtight container and stored in the fridge until
needed for your camping trip.

GRILLED SARDINES
WITH OLIVE TAPENADE AND FETA

SERVES 4

8–12 sardines

50 ml (2 fl oz/a good drizzle) extra-virgin olive oil, plus extra for rubbing

250 g (8 oz/1 cup) pitted black olives

3 tablespoons capers

4–6 anchovy fillets

Juice of ½ lemon

250 g (8 oz/1 cup) feta cheese, crumbled

Freshly ground black pepper

Enjoy this dish around a campfire with a glass of wine while the sun sets. The sardines are delicious served with a fresh crispy salad.

- -

1 Wash the sardines thoroughly, removing all scales and guts (you can leave the heads on, though).

2 Rub a little olive oil over the skin of the sardines.

3 Place the sardines on a hot barbecue grill and leave them to cook for about 10–15 minutes, turning 2–3 times during the cooking time.

4 Meanwhile, mince the olives, capers, anchovies, oil and lemon juice either in a food processor or a pestle and mortar. Blend or crush the ingredients together to form a paste, adding only pepper as a seasoning as all other ingredients are naturally salty.

5 You can tell the sardines have cooked if the eyes have turned white and the flesh flakes easily. Once the sardines are cooked, place them on 4 serving plates. Drizzle the tapenade over the fish and top with the feta cheese.

TRY SOMETHING DIFFERENT

• Try stuffing the inside of the sardines with fresh basil and pine nuts before wrapping in foil and cooking.

• Lay out a large double layer of foil and place 2-4 sardines in the centre. Wrap the foil around the fish to create a parcel. Repeat this with more foil and the remaining sardines to create 4 individual parcels. Cook the parcels under a hot grill or on a hot barbecue grill for the same amount of time.

BARBECUED TUNA

WITH LIME AND CHILLI

SERVES 4
Juice and zest of 1 lime
4 tablespoons olive oil
1 red chilli, deseeded and
  finely chopped
4 tuna steaks, weighing about
  125–150 g (4–5 oz) each
25 g (1 oz/about ½ a bunch)
  finely chopped coriander
Salt and pepper

TRY SOMETHING DIFFERENT

• You could also add
ginger and garlic to
the marinade.

• Adjust the amount of
chilli, depending on
how hot you like it!

• Cook the tuna steaks
in a frying pan on a
camping stove or on a
hot barbecue for the
same amount of time.

This recipe is perfect for the barbecue at home or even better on a beach surrounded by friends.

1 Mix the lime juice and zest, olive oil and chilli in a small bowl. Place the tuna steaks in a shallow dish and pour over the marinade, making sure the steaks are well covered. Season with salt and pepper. Cover and leave the tuna to marinate in the fridge or a cool box for about 10 minutes.

2 Lift the tuna steaks out of the marinade and place them directly on the hot barbecue grill. Cook for 10 minutes, turning halfway. Serve the steaks sprinkled with the fresh coriander. Remember it's fine to serve the tuna still a little pink in the middle as long as it was bought fresh.

TIP
Always make sure your barbecue is ready before you start preparing your ingredients and that you have hot, glowing embers ready for cooking.

FISH FINGER SANDWICH

From James May

SERVES 1

A drop of cooking oil
5 fish fingers
2 slices of stodgy white bread
Butter
A sauce of your choice –
    tomato, brown, salad
    cream etc.
Pepper

Scouting skills are so useful – such as map reading. If you learn to read symbols and contours, the map becomes a three-dimensional model, not just a sheet of paper. You can say, 'that must be a dip, that's going to have trees on it, that isn't and so on'.

JAMES MAY

1 Heat a bit of cooking oil in a hot frying pan. Bung the fish fingers in the pan – they should sizzle lightly. They will take about 6 minutes per side and the breadcrumbs should go a bit dark and crispy.

2 While this is going on, butter the 2 slices of bread. Smear 1 piece with your chosen sauce – I like salad cream or ketchup, and sometimes both.

3 Lay the cooked fish fingers on the butter-only slice of bread, 5 laid vertically and 1 across the top. Sprinkle with black pepper if you have it. Then press the saucey piece of bread firmly down on top.

4 Cut the sandwich in half vertically and enjoy.

CULLEN SKINK

From Richard Wilson

SERVES 4

1 kg (2 lb) smoked haddock
1 large onion, sliced
900 ml (1½ pints/3½ cups) milk
250 g (8 oz) mashed potato
50 g (2 oz) butter, cubed
1 tablespoon cream
Salt and pepper

This soup is perfect after a winter walk when you need something tasty and warming.

RICHARD WILSON

---

1 Put the smoked haddock in a saucepan with enough water to just cover it and simmer for about 5 minutes. Remove the fish, take out any bones and take off the skin.

2 Return the fish to the pan along with the onion and continue cooking for a further 15 minutes. Add the milk and bring to the boil. Add the mashed potato and stir to a creamy consistency. Add the butter, season to taste and add a little cream before serving.

ANGELS AND DEVILS ON HORSEBACK

SERVES 4

12 streaky smoked bacon rashers
12 fresh oysters (native or Rock), and out of their shell
12 soft D'agen soft prunes
Salt and pepper

YOU WILL ALSO NEED
Metal skewers

A fancy name for a very simple recipe; thankfully the ingredients are delicious.

---

1 Cut the bacon rashers in half and lay them out on a baking tray. Place 1 oyster on half the bacon rashers and 1 prune on the rest. Season with salt and pepper, roll up each angel and devil so the oysters and prunes are covered.

2 Secure the angels and devils on metal skewers and position them on a grid over glowing campfire embers. Cook for 3–4 minutes each side or until the bacon is crisp.

MUSSELS (AND SCALLOPS)

NICE AND SIMPLE

SERVES 4

2–3 kg (4–6 lb) mussels
4–8 large scallops, removed
from the shell (keep the
shell to cook them in)

YOU WILL ALSO NEED

1 large flat stone

TRY SOMETHING DIFFERENT

• You don't have to cook the
shellfish on a stone, why
not cook in a big pot over
a fire with a little white
wine, some butter, garlic
and parsley, until all the
mussels open wide.

• You could try using razor
clams and oysters as an
alternative to mussels and
scallops.

This is less of a recipe and more of a method of
cooking, which is perfect for the great outdoors,
especially if you're on the beach and the shellfish
is only minutes out of the sea. It also makes for
great communal eating.

1 Firstly make sure your campfire is really hot and that you
have glowing embers ready for cooking.

2 Place the large flat stone directly onto the campfire
embers and leave it for at least 1 hour to heat up – you can
put the stone on earlier in the day to get hot.

3 Prepare the mussels by washing in fresh water and pull
the beards off. Discard any mussels that are open and do
not shut when tapped.

4 Have your fishmonger prepare the scallops by removing
the stomach and gills (these are inedible) and place the
white flesh back into the shell for cooking.

5 When the large flat stone is hot, place the scallops directly
onto it. Leave them to cook for about 15 minutes and
then add the mussels. Leave the mussels and scallops to
cook for a further 10–15 minutes. (Alternatively place
the mussels end up directly into the embers (see photo
opposite) and watch them open.) The mussels will start
to jig around as they get hot, and will open wide when they
are cooked. Discard any mussels that have not opened after
cooking. These are both best enjoyed hot and with fresh
bread and butter.

Note: Always make sure shellfish is thoroughly cooked
before eating it, and if you're not sure about whether to
discard any before cooking it's always better to be safe than
sorry; trust your instincts.

ANTONY'S SPICED MACKEREL

From Antony Worrall Thompson

SERVES 8

8 mackerel fillets, weighing about 100 g (3½ oz) each

FOR THE SPICE PASTE

I tablespoon coriander seeds

I tablespoon black mustard seeds

I tablespoon cumin seeds

I teaspoon black peppercorns

I hot dried chilli, roughly chopped, deseeded if wished

I teaspoon salt

I tablespoon unrefined soft dark brown sugar

I've fond memories of being in the scouts. It was quite some time ago but I remember we had badges for cooking, how to tie knots (properly!), bob-a-job - of which I had the winning total for five years running - so I was quite good at it! They were happy days around the campfire with my fellow scouts. I'd recommend being a scout; it's more than just fun - it's part of a child's education.

ANTONY WORRALL THOMPSON

I To make the spice paste, heat a dry frying pan over a medium heat, then add the seeds and peppercorns and toast them, shaking from time to time for 2–3 minutes until the mustard seeds are popping and the spices are aromatic. Blend the toasted spices with the chilli to a smooth powder in a coffee grinder or using a pestle and mortar, or bowl and rolling pin. Combine the powder with the brown sugar and salt. Store in an airtight container until needed.

2 Lightly sprinkle both sides of each mackerel fillet with the spice mixture – about 2 teaspoons per fillet – and leave for about 30 minutes to marinate.

3 For ease of turning, place the fillets in a metal-hinged grill rack and cook on a hot barbecue for 1–2 minutes on each side until lightly charred and firm to the touch.

BE PREPARED Prepare the spice mixture at home to take with you. It can be stored in an airtight container in a cool, dark place for up to 3 months and used with any fish.

HOT ROAST SNAPPER

WITH COCONUT, CHILLI AND LIME SALSA
From Levi Roots

SERVES 8

3 kg (6 lb) snapper, either
   pink- or grey-skinned,
   gutted and scaled
1 lime

FOR THE STUFFING

1 small bunch of fresh
   coriander, finely chopped
1 small bunch of flat-leaf
   parsley, finely chopped
Leaves from 8 sprigs of
   thyme
Zest of 1 lime
Juice of 2 limes
4-cm (1½-inch) piece of
   fresh ginger, very finely
   chopped
1 hot red chilli (ideally
   Scotch bonnet), deseeded
   and finely chopped
5–6 tablespoons olive oil
Salt and pepper

FOR THE SALSA

250 g (8 oz) fresh coconut
   flesh
¼ teaspoon caster sugar
Juice of 8 limes
Zest of 2 limes
2 red chillies, deseeded and
   cut into fine slivers
Small bunch of fresh
   coriander leaves, coarsely
   chopped

When you're cooking outdoors it's all too easy to
make food that's just bland and filling. To me
that's a waste of the magical outdoor experience.
Remember, you have plenty of time, so why not
experiment with new herbs and spices, colours and
combinations. It will make your dish taste better
and brighten up your day.

LEVI ROOTS

1 Preheat the oven to 200°C (400°F), gas mark 6. Using
a very sharp knife, make 3 deep slashes on each side of
the fish. Squeeze the juice of a lime all over. Mix all the
stuffing ingredients together and stuff it into the slits and
the cavity.

2 Set the fish in a roasting tin lined with foil and roast in
the preheated oven, uncovered, for 45 minutes, by which
time the flesh closest to the bone at the thickest parts
should be perfectly white, not at all 'glassy' looking.

3 For the salsa use a potato peeler to make wafer-thin
shavings of coconut. Mix the sugar with the lime juice,
stirring until it dissolves, and toss the coconut with this
and all the other ingredients. Serve with the snapper.

TRY SOMETHING DIFFERENT

• Choose a smaller fish than
we have here (around 1-2 kg
/2-4 lb), stuff it, wrap it
in foil and cook it over
the glowing embers of a
campfire for 35-60 minutes
depending on size, turning
every 15 minutes or so to
ensure it cooks evenly.

THE KITCHEN IS THE HEART OF THE CAMP.

**PHILIP CARRINGTON,
SCOUT LEADER AND AUTHOR, 1918**

FRESH AIR AND FRESH VEGETABLES ARE A GREAT COMBINATION. THEY BOTH BRING A GREAT DEAL OF ENERGY, FUN AND COLOUR TO OUTDOOR DISHES. FROM MINTY SALADS AND RUSTIC SOUPS TO CREAMY RISOTTOS, THESE ARE STRICTLY NOT JUST FOR VEGETARIANS!

VEGETABLES AND SIDE DISHES

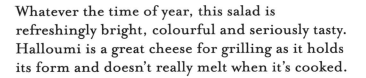

GRILLED HALLOUMI

WITH PEA, BROAD BEAN AND MINT SALAD

SERVES 4

400 g (13 oz) halloumi
   cheese, sliced about 1 cm
   (½ inch) thick
A drizzle of olive oil
150 g (5 oz) fresh peas
   (or frozen if fresh are
   unavailable)
150 g (5 oz) fresh broad
   beans (or frozen if fresh
   are unavailable)
A big handful of seasonal
   salad leaves, such as rocket,
   gem or endive, washed
25 g (1 oz/about ½ a bunch)
   fresh mint, roughly
   chopped
Juice of ½ lemon
Pepper

Whatever the time of year, this salad is refreshingly bright, colourful and seriously tasty. Halloumi is a great cheese for grilling as it holds its form and doesn't really melt when it's cooked.

1 Prepare your campfire, barbecue or grill. Coat the halloumi slices with a small amount of olive oil and season with ground black pepper.

2 If you are using fresh peas and broad beans, take them out of their pods, and then blanch them in boiling water for 3–4 minutes.

3 Place the halloumi straight onto a grill above the campfire or barbecue, and cook for about 5 minutes, turning halfway. Remove from the grill and leave to cool slightly.

4 Mix the lettuce leaves with the mint. You can either cut the cheese into cubes or leave as slices. In a big serving bowl place the minted salad leaves, top with the halloumi and then drizzle with lemon juice and olive oil.

BONITA'S MACARONI CHEESE

From Bonita Norris (youngest woman to climb Mount Everest)

SERVES 4-6

500 g (1 lb/2 cups) macaroni
Oil, for frying
100 g (3½ oz/⅓ cup)
    mascarpone cheese
150 g (5 oz) Cheddar cheese
8–12 cherry tomatoes
Parmesan cheese, for grating
1 small ball of mozzarella
    cheese
¼ of a nutmeg
Salt and pepper

Something like this is fantastic to eat when you get home if you've been out on a country hike, or even climbing a mountain! This is a great dish to cook and share with family and friends.

BONITA NORRIS

- -

1 Preheat your oven to 200°C (400°F), gas mark 6 or prepare a camp oven (see pages 22–5).

2 Cook the macaroni in a saucepan of lightly salted boiling water until just undercooked. Drain, but reserve some of the cooking water.

3 Heat some oil in a frying pan and fry the bacon or pancetta for 5–8 minutes, until crispy.

4 Add the cooked pasta to the frying pan, along with 2 tablespoons of the pasta's cooking water and the mascarpone. Once the mascarpone has melted to a sauce, grate in some extra cheddar cheese.

5 Tip the whole lot into an ovenproof dish and mix in the cherry tomatoes, season with salt and pepper and add grated Parmesan to the top along with torn-up strips of the mozzarella, and grate the nutmeg over the top.

6 Bake in the preheated or prepared camp oven for 10 minutes and finish off under the grill if possible to give a crispy topping.

VARIATION
Add cubed pancetta or chopped streaky bacon to make this into a meat dish.

BE PREPARED If you don't fancy preparing a camp oven, this is a perfect dish to be prepared at home and brought with you to reheat and enjoy on your first night at camp.

MEXICAN BEAN HOTPOT

WITH HOME-GROWN VEGGIES
From Joanne Smallman (youth leader)

SERVES 6

2 teaspoons oil

1 onion, chopped

2 garlic cloves, chopped or
  crushed

100–150 g (3½–5 oz) grated
  carrot

3 heaped teaspoons paprika
  (normal strength)

½ teaspoon chilli powder (or
  more if you like it hot)

1 heaped teaspoon cumin

1 x 400 g tin chopped
  tomatoes

500 ml (17 fl oz/2 cups)
  vegetable stock

2 tablespoons tomato ketchup

200 g (7 oz) courgette, cubed

100 g (3½ oz/2 handfuls)
  French beans, cut into 2.5-
  cm (1-inch) long pieces

1 x 400 g tin kidney beans,
  rinsed and drained

2 x 400 g tins beans —
  cannellini, chickpeas,
  borlotti (you choose!),
  rinsed and drained

Dash of Worcestershire
  sauce, to taste

TO SERVE

Rice or tortilla wraps

Soured cream

Grated cheese

This recipe is cheap, tasty and quick. Even when buying all the ingredients it's very reasonable per portion – and you'll save money by using your own produce. It can easily be multiplied to feed a crowd and it gets better with age – so the leftovers would be great for lunch!

1 Heat the oil in a big saucepan, add the onion and garlic and fry for a few minutes, until softened but not coloured.

2 Add the carrot to the pan and then the spices. Stir and fry for a further minute.

3 Add the tomatoes, stock and ketchup and reduce to a simmer. (This can be difficult on a campfire, but just keep adding small amounts of water if it's hot and evaporating quickly.)

4 Add the courgette, green beans, all of the tinned beans and the Worcestershire sauce. Give it a good stir and leave to simmer for 20 minutes, until the green beans are tender.

5 Enjoy the hotpot with rice or tortilla wraps, a splodge of soured cream and a sprinkle of cheese.

TRY SOMETHING DIFFERENT

• Make a side salad from mixed leaves and maybe some of your home-grown basil for a twist.

• This could also be cooked in a Dutch oven.

TRY SOMETHING DIFFERENT

• If you cannot find any dandelion leaves, you can replace them with rocket.

SERVES 4

200 g (7 oz/a large handful) fresh dandelion leaves

50 g (2 oz/a small handful) walnuts

10 g (½ oz) chives, chopped

4 tablespoons white wine vinegar

4 tablespoons olive oil OR 2 tablespoons walnut oil
   mixed with 2 tablespoons olive oil

250 g (8 oz/1 cup) cooked beetroot, cut into wedges

Salt and pepper

DANDELION, BEETROOT
AND WALNUT SALAD

An unusual combination of flavours, but one perfectly suited to enjoying in the great outdoors. Make sure you only pick the smaller (younger) dandelion leaves as the larger ones can be very bitter.

1 Thoroughly wash the dandelion leaves, especially if you have picked them from the wild.

2 Lightly roast the walnuts on a double layer of foil set over glowing campfire embers. Crush the roasted walnuts in a tea towel or plastic bag, giving it a whack with a bottle or rolling pin.

3 Mix the chopped chives, vinegar, oil and a little seasoning together in a small bowl.

4 Put all of the ingredients together in a serving bowl, but don't overmix because the beetroot will stain the salad leaves.

BALSAMIC ROASTED COURGETTES AND SHALLOTS

SERVES 4

2 large green or yellow
courgettes, sliced or diced
into cubes
8 small round shallots,
peeled and halved or
300 g (10 oz/1¼ cups) pearl
onions, peeled and left
whole
1–2 thyme sprigs
A drizzle of olive oil
2–3 tablespoons balsamic
vinegar
Salt and pepper

This is a great recipe to try at home on the barbecue. It is a perfect side dish to pair with the Pitted Chicken (see page 82) or the Spatchcock Chicken (see page 79). No need to use expensive balsamic vinegar and why not try using baby courgettes or even small button shallots.

1 Arrange the courgettes and shallots or onions on a double layer of foil.

2 Strip the thyme sprigs and sprinkle the leaves over the vegetables. Drizzle with a little olive oil, the balsamic vinegar and season generously. Fold over the corners of the foil and seal to form a parcel.

3 Place the foil parcel directly onto the glowing campfire embers. Leave to cook for 20–30 minutes, giving the parcel a shake about halfway through the cooking process.

TIP
Take extra care when opening the parcel as hot steam may shoot out of the foil.

CLASSIC CREAMY MUSHROOM RISOTTO

SERVES 4

Oil, for frying

1 onion, diced

1 garlic glove, finely crushed or diced

250 g (8 oz/1 cup) sliced mushrooms (my favourites for risotto are chestnut or porcini however, button mushrooms are fine)

350 g (11½ oz/½ cups) Arborio risotto rice

1.2 litres (2 pints/4 cups) hot vegetable stock made from stock cube

25 g (1 oz/a large knob) butter

25 g (1 oz/a good sprinkling) grated Parmesan cheese

25 g (1 oz) parsley, finely chopped

Salt and pepper

Risottos have grown in popularity over the years due to their flexibility and numerous variations. There's also something comforting about eating a hot creamy full-of-flavour risotto, especially on a chilly evening. This recipe gives you the flexibility to use any variety of mushroom, and also to make a healthier option if you've been enjoying your camp food just a little too much.

1 Heat a little oil in a medium, heavy-based saucepan over your campfire or a camping stove. Add the onion and garlic and cook for about 5 minutes, until softened. Add the mushrooms and fry for a further 2–3 minutes until browned.

2 Add the risotto rice and stir so that the rice is well coated with the oil and it begins to 'crack'.

3 Pour in a little hot stock and keep stirring until the liquid has all been absorbed. Gradually add all the liquid a small amount at a time, stirring, until the rice is plump, creamy and tender.

4 Season with salt and pepper and stir in the butter, Parmesan cheese and chopped parsley.

TRY SOMETHING DIFFERENT

• You can add diced cooked chicken breast for meat eaters or roasted red peppers.

• You can use dried mushrooms if fresh are not available.

POTATO, PEPPER AND CHERRY TOMATO
BAKED OMELETTE

SERVES 4

Oil, for greasing

250 g (8 oz/1 cup) diced
    cooked potatoes

1 pepper, deseeded and cut
    into strips

12–15 cherry tomatoes

150 g (5 oz/⅔ cups) hard
    cheese, grated (Cheddar or
    Gruyère are best)

5 eggs, beaten

200 ml (7 fl oz/1 cup) milk

Salt and pepper

This is a great recipe for using up leftover
potatoes or salad tomatoes from the day before.

1 Grease a 20-cm (8-inch) cake tin, deep frying pan or
deep ovenproof dish with a little oil.

2 Place the cooked potatoes, pepper and cherry tomatoes in
the dish and sprinkle over half the cheese.

3 Mix the beaten egg, milk and seasoning in a bowl or
measuring jug and then pour this over the vegetables.
Sprinkle the remaining cheese on top.

4 Cover the tin, pan or dish with foil and place it on the
edge of the glowing campfire embers. Leave it to cook for
about 40 minutes. Use a knife to check the egg is cooked all
the way through before cutting into wedges to serve.

TRY SOMETHING DIFFERENT

• Bake the tin or dish in a
conventional oven preheated
to 200°C (400°F), gas mark 6
for 20–25 minutes or until
just set.

• This dish can also be
cooked on a camping stove or
on a hot barbecue grill in a
large frying pan.

• There are so many other
flavours you can add to
this recipe – try using your
favourite vegetables and also
ingredients like pesto and
olives.

DUTCH RICE

From Carol Vorderman

SERVES 2

250 g (8 oz/1¼ cups) rice
1 heaped teaspoon Marmite
2–3 tablespoons vegetable oil
1 large onion, sliced
2 eggs, beaten
Soy sauce, to serve

Scouts are famous for cooking sausages around the campfire – I love cooking sausages on Bonfire Night and Lincolnshire sausages are definitely a favourite for me. The smell is fantastic. Here's a recipe that will go well with them.

CAROL VORDERMAN

1 Boil the rice using your own preferred method.

2 Dissolve the Marmite in a cupful of boiling water and stir well.

3 Heat the oil in a large frying pan and gently fry the sliced onions until softened.

4 Pour the beaten eggs over the mixture and allow the eggs to cook slowly, stirring constantly. Gradually add the cooked rice as you stir.

5 Add the Marmite and heat through for a minute or two. Turn down the heat and simmer the mixture until any excess moisture has evaporated.

6 Serve with soy sauce.

VARIATION

Turn this into a meat dish: remove the onions from the pan at the end of step 3, add 175 g (6 oz) trimmed and chopped bacon to the hot pan and fry for 5–8 minutes until crispy. Return the onions to the pan and continue from step 4.

FOIL-ROASTED SQUASH AND AUBERGINE

WITH ROSEMARY

SERVES 4

1 whole butternut squash
1 whole aubergine
2–3 rosemary stalks
A drizzle of olive oil
Salt and pepper

The aroma of roasted squash as you open the foil parcel with this recipe is really delicious. It's a feast for the eyes too, as the bright orange squash will have caramelised around the edges and will look too tempting to resist. It is delicious served with the Pitted Chicken (see page 82).

1 Halve the squash lengthways, scoop out the seeds and discard. Slice each half lengthways again into thick wedges. Cut the aubergine into long finger-like slices.

2 Strip the stalks of rosemary to release the leaves.

3 Mix the cut vegetables together, add the rosemary, season with salt and pepper and drizzle with olive oil (just enough to coat).

4 Arrange the vegetables on a double layer of foil, then fold the sides of the foil up and round to form a parcel.

5 Place the foil parcel directly onto the glowing campfire embers and leave to cook for about 40 minutes, giving the parcel a shake halfway through the cooking process.

TRY SOMETHING DIFFERENT

• Cook the foil parcel on a hot barbecue grill for the same amount of time as the main recipe.

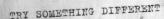

TRY SOMETHING DIFFERENT

• Adjust the chilli in this recipe to suit your palate.

• Alternatively, make it a meat dish by replacing the couscous or rice with minced pork or beef.

• Cook the foil package on a hot barbecue grill for the same amount of time.

SERVES 1

1 green pepper

50 g (2 oz/⅓ cup) cooked couscous or rice

50 g (2 oz/⅓ cup) breadcrumbs or crumbled
  crackers

5–10 dashes of Tabasco sauce

1 teaspoon smoked paprika

½ garlic clove, finely chopped

MEXICALI PEPPERS

If you like spicy food, then this little firecracker will be right up your street. Add Tabasco sauce according to personal taste.

- -

1 Slice the top off the pepper and remove the seeds.

2 Boil some water in a saucepan and parboil the pepper for about 5 minutes. Leave it to cool slightly.

3 Mix the cooked couscous or rice and breadcrumbs or crackers with the Tabasco sauce, paprika and garlic.

4 Fill the pepper with the couscous mixture, place the pepper on a double layer of foil and fold the sides up and around the pepper, twisting the top to seal.

5 Place the foil package directly onto the glowing campfire embers and leave to cook for about 30 minutes.

POTATO CAKES

From Phillip Schofield

SERVES 4
400–500 g (13 oz–1 lb)
   potatoes, peeled and diced
150 ml (¼ pint/½ cup) milk
50–75 g (2–3 oz/4–6
   tablespoons) butter
150 g (5 oz/½ cup) self-
   raising flour
Salt and pepper

TRY SOMETHING DIFFERENT
• Cook the potato cakes
on a baking tray in
a conventional oven
preheated to 150°C
(300°F), gas mark 2 for
the same amount of time.

Sometimes you just need something comforting, filling and easy to make. This is ideal.

1 Bring a saucepan of lightly salted water to the boil and cook the potatoes until cooked.

2 Drain the potatoes and mash them adding lots of milk, butter and seasoning to taste.

3 Add enough self-raising flour to make a stiff dough.

4 Divide the dough into 4 portions and shape each portion into a flat pattie shape about 1 cm (½ inch) deep.

5 Place the potato cakes on a baking tray or on a double layer of foil and place on the edge of the glowing campfire embers. Leave to cook for about 15–20 minutes until golden brown.

THERE'S MUCH MORE TO CAMPING DESSERTS THAN JUST MARSHMALLOWS (ALTHOUGH THERE'S NOTHING WRONG WITH THEM; TRY MY RECIPE FOR TOASTED MARSHMALLOWS AND JELLY BABIES ON PAGE 157). FROM GRILLED PINEAPPLE WITH RUM SYRUP (SEE PAGE 154) TO A CLASSIC LIKE CAMP DOUGHNUTS (SEE PAGE 149), HERE ARE SOME STICKY TREATS THAT ALWAYS TASTE GREAT IN THE OPEN AIR.

SWEET THINGS

JAMBOREE JAM

MAKES ABOUT 700 g (1 lb 6 oz)

450 g (14½ oz/3½ cups) mixed berries (hulled strawberries, blackberries, raspberries and blueberries), fresh or frozen

500 g (1 lb/2¼ cups) jam or preserving sugar (see Note)

YOU WILL ALSO NEED
Sterilised jars and lids

This is a really easy jam recipe that is perfect for making on a rainy day in camp. Great paired with pancakes or simply spread on fresh bread.

1 Put the mixed berries in a large pan and mash with a fork to release the juices. Put the pan over a medium heat either on the campfire or camp stove. Cook the berries for about 10–15 minutes, until softened.

2 Add the jam or preserving sugar and bring to the boil. When it begins to bubble vigorously and the bubbles rise to the edge of the pan and cannot be stirred down, leave to boil like this for 4½ minutes then take off the heat.

3 Leave the jam to cool slightly and then pour into your sterilised jars. Seal and refrigerate until needed. The jam will keep for up to 1 month stored in a cool, dark place.

Note: Jam or preserving sugars are special varieties of sugar with added pectin to help jam and jellies set.

BE PREPARED Make plenty of this jam in advance to take with you on your camping trip – perfect for early morning jam on toast.

MAKES 4
4 eating apples
200 g (7 oz/I cup) caster sugar
I tablespoon cinnamon or nutmeg

TOFFEE APPLES

These bring back memories of summer fairs and Bonfire Night. The combination of the hot cooked apple and hard sugar is impossible to resist...

I Make sure the apples are well washed and dried. Place each apple onto a peeled green stick (see page 94) or wooden skewer and hold over glowing campfire embers until the peel is scorched (but not burnt). Remove from the fire and scrape off the peel.

2 Make up a mixture of the sugar and either cinnamon or nutmeg and roll the apples in it until they are completely covered.

3 Rotate the apples over the glowing embers until the sugar melts to form a glaze. Then remove from the fire, place them on a sheet of foil and leave to cool and set before eating.

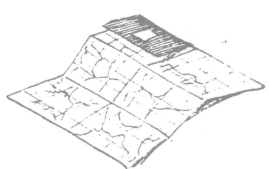

MAKES 6 OATCAKES

250 g (8 oz/1 cup) oatmeal or porridge oats
1 teaspoon salt
1 teaspoon baking powder
10 g (½ tablespoon) Demerara sugar
1 tablespoon butter or margarine, melted
Hot water

OATCAKES

This dessert has wholesome oats as one of its main ingredients. If you'd rather enjoy a savoury oatcake, then simply leave the sugar out to make a tasty cracker to enjoy with cheese.

1 Mix three-quarters of the oatmeal with the salt, baking powder and sugar in a mixing bowl. Add the melted butter and stir through. Add a very small amount of water to bind the mix together.

2 Knead the dough into a round shape on a sheet of foil lightly dusted with flour. Roll the dough out on the sheet of foil into a large sausage shape. Rub the remaining oats into the surface of the dough and then cut it into 6 slices.

3 Place the cakes onto a double layer of foil and place it directly on the edge of the glowing campfire embers for about 8–10 minutes, turning halfway, until the edges of the cakes start to curl. You could secure the oatcakes on skewers and finish off the browning over the fire if preferred.

CHOCOLATE ORANGE

SERVES 1

1 large orange
3 wafer-thin peppermint-
   filled chocolates

This is just as much fun to make as it is to eat!

1 Slice the orange in half across the middle and remove as many pips as possible.

2 Lay the 3 wafer-thin chocolates on one half of the orange then place the other half on top.

3 Wrap the orange in a double layer of foil and place it directly on the glowing campfire embers for 10–15 minutes, turning frequently. Carefully unwrap the orange and enjoy with a spoon (as you would eat a grapefruit).

CAMP CRUNCHIES

MAKES 15 BARS

200 g (7 oz/¾ cup) dried
   apricots

65 g (2½ oz/10 tablespoons)
   sultanas

400 g (13 oz/2 cups) puffed
   rice cereal

100 g (3½ oz/⅓ cup) icing
   sugar

50 g (2 oz/8 tablespoons)
   toasted sesame seeds

1 tablespoon honey or golden
   syrup

100 g (3½ oz/a large knob)
   butter or margarine,
   melted, plus extra for
   greasing

This is a great way to get a lot of very healthy ingredients inside you without really realising it. Great for picnics or family barbecues.

1 Cut each apricot into 8 pieces and mix all the dry ingredients together in a bowl.

2 Stir in the honey or syrup and butter or margarine and mix well.

3 Spread the mixture out onto a greased baking tray or a double layer of foil.

4 Leave this to set hard overnight in your fridge or cool box (or best possible way of cooling available to you while camping!). Once set, cut the camp crunchies into bars or squares.

TRY SOMETHING DIFFERENT

• Try using chocolate
spread or peanut
butter instead of
the strawberry jam.

MAKES 8 DOUGHNUTS

8 slices bread

Strawberry jam (preferably homemade), for
    spreading

1 egg, beaten

6 tablespoons milk

6 tablespoons flour

5–6 tablespoons vegetable oil

Caster sugar, for coating

CAMP DOUGHNUTS

The great thing about these doughnuts is that they are
square instead of round. The trick is to fry them until they
are really crispy – no one likes a soggy doughnut. Once
you've had one of these you'll want another, then another.

1 Spread 3 slices of bread with jam, pile them on top of each other
and then top with a fourth slice. Repeat with the other 4 slices of
bread to make 2 layered stacks.

2 Trim the crusts off each stack and cut each stack into 4 quarters to
make 8 squares.

3 Mix the egg and milk together in a shallow bowl and gradually add
the flour (this will help you avoid having a lumpy batter).

4 Heat a little oil in a non-stick pan, dip each doughnut square in the
batter and fry for about 5 minutes on each side, until crispy.

5 Put the caster sugar in a shallow bowl and dip in each doughnut to
coat it in sugar while they are still warm. Serve immediately.

FOR ALL WHO TAKE **DELIGHT** IN THE FREE LIFE OF CAMP IN AIR-SWEET APPETITE AND IN THE **DREAMLESS** SLEEP THAT FALLS ON THE WIND-SWEPT BRAIN.

THIS BOOK IS WRITTEN

**LINCOLN GREEN,
'CAMP COOKERY FOR SCOUTS', 1914**

HOT CROSS BUNS

MAKES ABOUT 6 BUNS
250 g (8 oz/1⅔ cups) self-
  raising flour
60 g (2 oz/10 tablespoons)
  brown sugar
A pinch of mixed spice
2 eggs, beaten
250 ml (8 fl oz/1 cup) milk
60 g (2 oz/10 tablespoons)
  butter or margarine,
  melted, plus extra for
  greasing

Here is a delicious snack that can be enjoyed all year round.

1 Preheat the oven to 180°C (350°F), gas mark 4. Mix the dry ingredients together in a bowl. Add the eggs, milk and melted butter, mixing until it forms a smooth batter.

2 Using a smooth pebble as a mould, shape pieces of foil around the pebble to make 8 foil dishes, greasing them well with butter or margarine. Divide the batter into the foil dishes (they should not be more than one-third full). Make a cross on the top of the buns.

3 Bake the foil dishes in the preheated oven for 20 minutes.

BE PREPARED These buns are best made at home and are ideal for taking on a picnic.

SHERBET APPLES

SERVES 4
2 apples
250 g (8 oz/1¼ cup) icing
  sugar
1 teaspoon bicarbonate of
  soda
1 teaspoon tartaric acid
  (available in supermarkets
  or pharmacies)

Perfect if you find toffee apples too sticky.

1 Peel and core the apples and cut them into thin slices. Place the apple slices in a foil bag with a little water. Seal the bag and place it directly on the glowing campfire embers. Leave to cook for about 15 minutes.

2 Mix the remaining ingredients together in a bowl. When the apple is cooked, divide it between 4 bowls and serve with a sprinkling of the sherbet mix.

SUMMER PUDDING

SERVES 4

500 g (1 lb/2 cups) mixed
    fresh berries (hulled
    strawberries, blackberries,
    blueberries or raspberries)
200 g (7 oz/1 cup) caster
    sugar
6–10 slices stale bread
Clotted cream or double
    cream, to serve

TRY SOMETHING DIFFERENT

• As an alternative, try
scooping out a small
loaf of brioche and
filling with the cooked
berry mixture, or even
just serving the fruit
with clotted cream.

This is a very refined recipe made with some very commonplace ingredients. Give it a try and surprise yourself.

1 Put the fruit and sugar in a saucepan and add enough water to just cover the fruit. Cook over a medium heat for about 10–15 minutes, until the fruit is soft and beginning to break up.

2 Remove the crusts from the stale bread and place a layer of bread in the bottom of a glass or plastic bowl.

3 In alternate layers, spoon fruit on the bread, then cover with another slice of bread and repeat the process, ending with a slice of bread on top. Remember to press down firmly after each layer.

4 Cover the bread with a layer of foil and put something heavy enough to compress the pudding on top. Leave overnight in a cool box or fridge.

5 Serve with fresh clotted cream or double cream.

SERVES 6-8

1 whole fresh pineapple

100 ml (3½ fl oz/⅓ cup) water

100 g (3½ oz/½ cup) caster sugar

A drizzle of dark rum (use as much or as little
as you like)

Juice of ½ lime

GRILLED PINEAPPLE
WITH RUM SYRUP

Fresh pineapple served in an unusual way with a little bit
of a kick.

1 Peel and core the pineapple and then cut into chunky rings about
2.5 cm (1 inch) thick.

2 Mix the water, sugar, rum and lime juice together in a saucepan
and bring to the boil. Continue to cook for about 10 minutes until it
forms a syrupy consistency.

3 Place the pineapple slices directly on the hot grill of a barbecue and
grill each side for about 5 minutes or until caramelised, basting the
pineapple with the syrup throughout the cooking time.

4 Serve with more syrup poured over the top and enjoy.

COCONUT MAGIC PIE

SERVES 4

4 eggs, beaten

200 g (7 oz/1 cup) plain flour

250 ml (8 fl oz/1 cup) milk

2 tablespoons vanilla essence

100 g (3½ oz/a large knob)
  margarine or butter

100 g (3½ oz/½ cup) caster
  sugar

200 g (7 oz/1 cup) desiccated
  coconut

The magic pie is so called because as it is cooked, the flour settles to form a crusty base, and the coconut rises to make the topping, leaving an egg custard in the middle.

1 Preheat the oven to 170°C (325°F), gas mark 3. Put the eggs in a bowl and gradually stir in the flour. Mix in the rest of the ingredients and pour the mixture into a shallow ovenproof dish.

2 Bake the pie in the preheated oven for about 1 hour or until the centre of the pie is firm.

BE PREPARED This is ideally made at home and taken with you on your trip. The pie will keep for 2–3 days once cooked.

SWEET KEBABS

SERVES 4

1 apple

2 oranges or 1 grapefruit, cut
  into segments

12 cherries

12 marshmallows

YOU WILL ALSO NEED

A green stick (see page 94) or
  soaked wooden skewers

Be warned, these will be very hot.

1 Cut the apple and oranges or grapefruit into several pieces large enough to put onto a skewer without splitting.

2 Make a skewer from a green stick or use soaked wooden skewers. Skewer your chosen selection of fruit on the stick or skewer, leaving the marshmallows aside.

3 Cook the kebabs over the glowing campfire embers for 5–10 minutes. Add the marshmallows and cook for a further 2 minutes, turning frequently until browned.

TOASTED MARSHMALLOWS

AND JELLY BABIES

**SERVES AS MANY
AS YOU WANT!**

Lots of marshmallows

YOU WILL ALSO NEED

Long thin green sticks (see
page 94), sharpened to
a point, with the bark
removed (you will need
I per person) — you could
also use a toasting fork

So again, this is not exactly a recipe, but who
can go camping and not toast a marshmallow?
Remember to leave the marshmallows and jelly
babies to cool before putting them in your mouth.

I Place your marshmallow on the end of your stick and
position it just over the glowing campfire embers or over
the barbecue. Gradually rotate the stick to toast the whole
marshmallow. This should only take I minute depending
on how close your marshmallow is to the fire. Be careful
when you eat it, it will be HOT.

TRY SOMETHING DIFFERENT

• Why not try putting a
jelly baby on the green
stick instead and gently
toasting until it goes
really soft. You'll find
when you eat it the
centre of the jelly baby
has gone liquid!

• How about dipping your
toasted marshmallow in
melted chocolate for an
extra sweet treat.

APPLE AND RHUBARB ALMOND SPONGE

From Richard Branson

SERVES 4

450 g (14½ oz) cooking
  apples, peeled, cored and
  sliced
450 g (14½ oz) rhubarb,
  washed and cut into
  2.5-cm (1-inch) pieces
Grated zest and juice of
  1 orange
90 g (3¼ oz/½ cup)
  Demerara sugar
60 g (2¼ oz/⅓ cup) sultanas

FOR THE SPONGE

90 g (3¼ oz/⅓ cup) butter
90 g (3¼ oz/½ cup) caster
  sugar
2 eggs, beaten
A few drops of almond
  essence
90 g (3¼ oz/½ cup) self-
  raising flour
25 g (1 oz/⅓ cup) ground
  almonds
Salt
A little milk
Flaked almonds, for
  sprinkling

Scouting – great fun, great adventures. Lots of
outdoor activities which I love and valuable
experience of leadership.

RICHARD BRANSON

- -

1 Preheat the oven to 180°C (350°F), gas mark 4.

2 Put the apples and rhubarb in a saucepan and add the
orange zest and juice, sugar and sultanas. Cook over a
gentle heat and simmer for about 15 minutes. Pour into a
greased ovenproof dish.

3 To make the sponge topping, cream together the butter
and sugar in a mixing bowl. Add the eggs and almond
essence. Mix in the flour, ground almonds and salt. Add a
little milk, if necessary, to make a dropping consistency.

4 Spoon the sponge mixture on top of the fruit and
sprinkle the top with flaked almonds.

5 Bake in the preheated oven for 35–40 minutes until
golden on top.

BE PREPARED Bake this at home and take with you for afternoon tea on your first day.

HONEY BUNS

From Stephen Fry

MAKES 12 SMALL BUNS

2 eggs

75 g (3 oz/⅓ cup) caster sugar

I teaspoon soft dark sugar

90 g (3¼ oz/⅔ cup) self-
raising flour, sifted

I teaspoon baking powder

A pinch of salt

90 g (3¼ oz/⅓ cup) melted
butter, cooled

I tablespoon honey

YOU WILL ALSO NEED

Paper cake cases

I think that the principles that Scouting started
with are as important today as they ever were.
They're not saying you have to be heroes, or you
have to be giants. They say you have to be kind,
be considerate, be thoughtful and you have to push
yourself. And if there's any better advice for any
young person I've yet to hear it.

STEPHEN FRY

I Preheat the oven to 180°C (350°F), gas mark 4.

2 Whisk together the eggs and both sugars in a mixing
bowl. Fold in the sifted flour, baking powder and salt.
Leave the mixture to rest for about 30 minutes.

3 Stir in the melted butter and honey.

4 Spoon the mixture into paper cake cases, filling them
about three-quarters full. Bake in the preheated oven for
about 25 minutes.

BE PREPARED Bake these delicious buns at home to enjoy at camp. They are also a
perfect in-car treat for your journey.

BAKED CHOCOLATE BANANAS

SERVES 5

5 bananas

5–6 chunks of chocolate per
banana

Anyone who has been a scout or guide will
remember this from their childhood camping trips.

1 Leave the bananas in their skins and slice them open
lengthways, taking care not to cut all the way through to
the bottom.

2 Place small pieces or chunks of chocolate into the bananas
all the way along.

3 Wrap each banana in foil and place them directly onto
the glowing campfire embers or on a hot barbecue grill for
about 10 minutes – just enough time for the bananas to go
soft and the chocolate to melt.

TRY SOMETHING DIFFERENT

• Try different
flavoured chocolate
or use jam or honey.

CAMEMBERT AND BLACKBERRIES

From Peter Sidwell (chef and TV presenter)

SERVES 4

2 Camemberts
1 handful of blackberries or
    blueberries
2 large sprigs of rosemary
25 g (1 oz/a large knob)
    butter, softened

I loved being a scout. It was a huge part of my life growing up – it may even have kick-started my cooking career as one of my first cooking memories as a kid was cooking Dampers (see page 67) in the scouts. I also remember making our own ovens using a Dutch oven and digging it into the ground and building a small fire underneath it to bake bread and Cowboy Dinner (see page 101).

Don't worry about getting your fingers sticky with this recipe – it's worth it!

PETER SIDWELL

1 Unwrap a Camembert and push blackberries or blueberries into the top, through the skin (6–8 berries per cheese should do).

2 Place a good sprig of rosemary in the centre of a piece of foil, cut to about 30 cm (12 inches) square. Brush the foil with the butter and place the Camembert on top, lifting up the edge of the foil to form a parcel around the cheese. Finally bring the corners of the foil together at the top and pinch together to form a type of handle. Repeat for the second Camembert.

3 Place the cheeses in the corners of the glowing campfire embers or the corner of a hot barbecue grill, where it is not too hot, and cook for about 10 minutes until the cheese is soft in the middle. Serve with crostini for dipping.

SERVES 6-8
500 g (1 lb) chilled ready-made pastry of your choice

OXYGEN TART

From Michael Palin

This is a truly Monty Python-esque dish. A real breath of fresh air...

1 Roll out the pastry on a sheet of lightly floured foil.

2 Make the pastry into a base and top with nothing at all.

3 Cook on the glowing campfire embers for 10–15 minutes

VARIATION
For special occasions, walnuts may be added, turning it into an oxygen and walnut tart.

EVERY GOOD OUTDOOR MEAL SHOULD HAVE AN EQUALLY GOOD DRINK TO ACCOMPANY IT. WHETHER IT IS A SUMMER REFRESHER OR A WINTER WARMER, THEY ARE ALWAYS BEST ENJOYED OUTDOORS.

DRINKS

ELDERFLOWER CORDIAL

MAKES 2 LITRES

20 elderflower heads (in full bloom)

1.2 litres (2 pints/4½ cups) water

1.75 kg (3½ lb/nearly 2 packets or 6–7 enamel mugs full) caster sugar

2 lemons, sliced

75 g (3 oz/a large pinch) citric acid (available from supermarkets or pharmacies)

This cordial will last for about 2 months, so it's perfect for helping to hang onto those summer holiday memories during the autumn months.

- -

1 Thoroughly wash and pick over the elderflower heads, making sure there are no bugs lurking in the flowers.

2 Mix the water and sugar together in a large saucepan and bring to the boil. Simmer for 10 minutes to form a syrup.

3 Mix the lemon slices with the elderflower heads – rub them together well and then add them to the sugar syrup in the saucepan along with the citric acid. Cover and leave to infuse for 1 hour.

4 Pour the mixture through a clean tea towel or muslin cloth into a large bowl. Decant the liquid into screw-top containers (which have been sterilised in hot water) or bottle and store either in a fridge or a cool dark place.

5 Best enjoyed with soda water and fresh mint over ice.

BE PREPARED Make ahead at home and bring with you to camp.

CAMPING GINGER BEER

MAKES 6-8 DRINKS

1.5 litres (2½ pints/6 cups) water

500 g (1lb/a 20–25-cm (8–10-inch) piece) fresh ginger, peeled and finely chopped

250 g (8 oz/1 cup) light brown sugar

1 lime, cut into 6–8 wedges

If you find the gingery kick too much just reduce the quantities slightly.

1 Put the water and ginger in a large saucepan and bring to the boil. Take the saucepan off the heat, cover and leave to infuse for a minimum of 12 hours, preferably 24 hours.

2 Once infused, pass through a sieve and return the liquid to the saucepan. Add the sugar, return to the heat and stir until the sugar dissolves. Remove from the heat and leave to cool. Decant into sterilised screw-top bottles, keep cool (ideally refrigerated) and store for up to 4 days. Serve over crushed ice with a wedge of lime or some added lime juice.

ICED APPLE AND RASPBERRY TEA

SERVES 6-8

1.5 litres (2½ pints/6 cups) water

5 teabags (preferably English breakfast or Earl Grey)

125 g (6 tablespoons) clear runny honey

500 ml (17 fl oz/2 cups) freshly squeezed apple juice (not from concentrate)

150 g (5 oz/½ cup) raspberries, plus extra to serve

1 dessert apple, to serve

This is so refreshing, especially if you've come back from a day hiking or just lying on the beach.

1 Put all of the ingredients together in a large saucepan and bring to the boil. Cover and leave to brew for 2–4 minutes.

2 Pour the liquid through a clean tea towel or muslin cloth into a large bowl. Decant into a sterilised screw-top bottle and chill for up to 3 days.

3 Serve the tea very chilled (find the best way of chilling while camping such as in a cool box or a nice farmer's fridge!) with more fresh raspberries and slices of apple.

PRACTICALLY
THE ONLY THING
YOU CAN'T TAKE INTO
THE GREAT
OUTDOORS
IS A MICROWAVE
AND WHO NEEDS ONE
OF THOSE?

NICK ALLEN

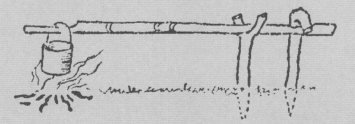

SERVES 10

2 kg (4 lb) rhubarb stalks, chopped
2 litres (3½ pints/8 cups) water
2 tablespoons grated lemon zest
5 tablespoons lemon juice
200 g (7 oz/1 cup) caster sugar

RHUBARB CORDIAL

Rhubarb is no longer something to be endured at your grandmother's house; it's a delicious, versatile ingredient that has come right back into fashion. This beats orange or blackcurrant cordial hands down.

1 Put the rhubarb, water and lemon zest and juice together in a large saucepan and bring to the boil. Leave to simmer over a gentle heat for 20–30 minutes.

2 Pass the liquid through a clean tea towel or muslin cloth into a large bowl. Save the cooked rhubarb for another dish and return the strained liquid to the saucepan.

3 Add the sugar to the saucepan and bring to the boil. Simmer for 10–15 minutes to form a syrupy consistency.

4 Take off the heat, leave to cool and then decant into a sterilised screw-top jar or bottle. Keep cool (ideally refrigerated) for up to 5 days. Best served cold with lemonade and a slice of lime.

BE PREPARED Make this cordial at home, store in sterilised bottles and bring it with you to camp.

NETTLE, LEMON AND APPLE JUICE

SERVES 4

500 ml (17 fl oz/2 cups)
   freshly squeezed apple juice
   (not from concentrate)
500 ml (17 fl oz/2 cups) water
150 g (5 oz/⅔ cup) sugar
½ a shopping bag-full of
   fresh nettle leaves (see
   page 52)
100 ml (3½ fl oz/6
   tablespoons) lemon juice

Here's a drink that will revive the weariest of spirits. Use only the young, top leaves of the nettle plant, as these are the most tender.

1 Put the apple juice, water and sugar in a large saucepan and bring to the boil. Simmer for 10 minutes to form a syrupy consistency.

2 Roughly chop the nettle leaves (taking care to wear gloves) and add them to the syrup. Add the lemon juice, mix well, cover and leave to infuse for 20 minutes.

3 Pass the liquid through a clean tea towel or muslin cloth into a large bowl and decant the juice into a sterilised screw-top jar or bottle. Keep cool (ideally refrigerated) for up to 3 days.

CHERRY LEMONADE

SERVES 4

125 ml (4 fl oz/½ cup) lemon
   juice
1 litre (1¾ pints/4 cups)
   water
100 g (3½ oz/½ cup) caster
   sugar
200 g (7 oz/1 cup)
   maraschino cherries
Soda water, to top up

Just when you thought lemonade couldn't get any sweeter...

1 Put the lemon juice, water and sugar in a large saucepan and bring to the boil. Simmer for about 15 minutes to form a syrupy consistency.

2 Add the cherries and leave to simmer for 2–3 minutes. Take off the heat and leave to cool with the cherries in the syrup. Strain to remove the cherries if you'd prefer or leave them in and then add to soda water (1 part syrup to 4 parts soda water) to serve.

MAKES ABOUT 6-8 DRINKS
1 litre (1¾ pints/4 cups) milk
500 ml (17 fl oz/2 cups) water
8–10 heaped tablespoons instant hot chocolate
    powder (or as much as you want!)
1 x 1-kg carton ready-to-use custard
A large handful of mini marshmallows

CAMP HOT CHOCOLATE

This is the one thing that brings back memories of years of being a scout and camping. This recipe was finely tweaked over many trips by many scout leaders. It's sweet and thick and chocolatey. Serve this just before bed with extra marshmallows and whipped cream on top. Why not try using different flavoured hot chocolate powder?

1 Put the milk and water in a large saucepan and bring to the boil. Add the hot chocolate powder and stir well to get rid of any lumps.

2 Pour in the custard and bring back to the boil over a gentle heat, being careful not to burn the bottom of the pan. Drop in the marshmallows and stir until melted. Serve immediately.

SPICED COFFEE

SERVES 4

4 tablespoons ground coffee (use whichever is your favourite, but for this drink, the stronger the better)

½ teaspoon ground cinnamon

½ teaspoon ground all-spice

400 ml (14 fl oz/ 1½ cups) boiling water

1 tablespoon caramel dessert syrup

400 ml (14 fl oz/1½ cups) milk

The distinctive spicy aroma of this drink is reminiscent of walking through a market in Marrakech. Bring the essence of Morocco to your camping trip.

1 Mix the ground coffee, cinnamon and all-spice together in a large bowl.

2 Pour over the boiling water, cover and leave to brew for 30–60 seconds. Stir in the caramel syrup. Add milk to taste and enjoy.

TRY SOMETHING DIFFERENT

• Try chilling the coffee once it's made in the fridge or a cool box and serve it over ice.

• Add different flavoured syrups to the coffee or different blends of ground coffee to get varied results.

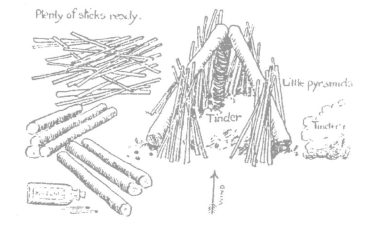

Plenty of sticks ready.

Little pyramids

Tinder

Tinder

WIND

MINTY MOJITO

8 tablespoons Demerara
    sugar
4 limes, 2 cut into wedges
    and 2 juiced
1 bunch of mint
400 ml (14 fl oz/1½ cups)
    dark or white rum
1 litre (1¾ pints/4 cups)
    sparkling water or
    lemonade

The history of the mojito goes as far back as Sir Francis Drake in the 1500s. It has five key ingredients: white rum, sugar, lime, sparkling water and mint. The name mojito is thought to have come from the word *mojo*, which is an old Cuban seasoning made from lime. It's a great cocktail to make in a pitcher and share around with adult friends.

1 Put the sugar, juice of 2 of the limes and a little water in a large saucepan and bring to the boil. Simmer for 10–15 minutes to form a syrupy consistency.

2 Put some ice, the lime wedges, mint leaves and the rum in a large jug. Pour over the sugar syrup and top up with sparkling water or lemonade. Stir well and serve the mojito in chilled glasses.

HOMEMADE NETTLE BEER

**MAKES 3 LITRES
(5 PINTS)**

1 kg (2 lb/ 4 cups) freshly
  picked nettle leaves (see
  page 52)
3 litres (5 pints/ 12 cups)
  water
225 g (7½ oz/1 cup)
  Demerara sugar
2 teaspoons ground ginger
1 x 7-g sachet of fresh yeast
1 white bread slice, toasted

Here's one to surprise your friends with on your
first night camping. It might not sting, but it
certainly packs a punch! I'm not sure how strong
this beer is, but it has an alluring, unusual flavour
– it's definitely worth a try!

1 Put the nettles and water in a large saucepan, bring to the
boil and simmer for about 30 minutes.

2 Pass the liquid through a clean tea towel or muslin cloth
into a large bowl.

3 Add the sugar and ground ginger to the nettle stock,
return to the saucepan and simmer for 10–15 minutes until
the sugar has dissolved.

4 Decant the liquid into a sterilised brewing pan or
container. Spread the fresh yeast on top of the small piece
of toast and float it carefully on top of the liquid.

5 Seal or cover the pan or container
and leave it in a cool, dry place
indoors for 3 days, making sure the
temperature does not fluctuate
too much. Keep cool (ideally
refrigerated) for up to 1 week.

BE PREPARED Make this at home
to take with you on camp.

ADMIT IT, YOU CAN'T SPEND ALL YOUR TIME COOKING AND EATING (MUCH AS YOU WOULD LIKE TO). HERE ARE SOME GREAT IDEAS FOR OUTDOOR ACTIVITIES WHETHER YOU'RE CAMPING OR SIMPLY PLANNING A DAY OUT. THE GREAT OUTDOORS IS THE WORLD'S BEST ADVENTURE PLAYGROUND. AND, WAIT FOR IT, MOST ACTIVITIES WILL COST YOU NOTHING AT ALL . . .

OUTDOOR
ACTIVITIES

10 OUTDOOR ACTIVITIES YOU CAN DO FOR NOTHING

1. Get on your bike

Visit the Sustrans website to find out more about the National Cycle Network and its more than 10,000 miles of walking and cycle routes. www.sustrans.org.uk

2. Go for a walk in a National Park

Home to some of the most breathtaking and spectacular landscapes in Britain, why not go for a walk in one of our 14 National Parks. www.nationalparks.gov.uk

3. Go to a festival

Britain has a whole host of free local festivals that happen all year round. www.efestivals.co.uk

4. Go to the beach

With more than 3,300 British beaches and marinas now displaying the Blue Flag quality indicator, there's nothing to stop you grabbing your swimming costume and heading to the sea. www.blueflag.org.uk

5. Go for a dip

The Outdoor Swimming Society believes it's time to get back to the joy of swimming under an open sky. Membership is free. www.outdoorswimmingsociety.com

6. Go bird watching

Why not take your kids into the garden or a nearby park and see how many of the over 450 recorded species of bird in the UK they can spot. The RSPB or British Garden Birds websites can help them identify what they saw. www.rspb.org.uk www.garden-birds.co.uk

7. Go star gazing

The BBC's Sky at Night website has sky maps and constellation guides to get you started. www.bbc.co.uk/skyatnight

8. Go on a walking tour

You don't have to head to the countryside to go for a walk. Britain's cities are home to some fantastic world-class architecture, and now lots of towns and cities offer free local walking tours. The Ramblers' website lists a variety of urban walks. www.ramblers.org.uk/INFO/urbanwalks.html

9. Fly a kite

Keep kids entertained on a windy day by making and flying a kite. www.making-and-flying-kites.com

10. Renew a local space

You know that bit of land you walk past every day and think someone should really clean that up and make it wonderful for all the wildlife and people round here? Now's your chance to do it yourself. Get a group of volunteers together and ask your local council for permission to get started.

10 THINGS YOU CAN DO OUTDOORS TODAY

1. Join Scouting

The Scout Association provides challenge and adventure for 400,000 boys and girls aged 6–25. If you're older than that don't worry – adult volunteers are always welcome to help make Scouting more widely available in the UK's communities. www.scouts.org.uk

2. Visit a children's farm

From watching an egg hatch and cradling a baby chick to riding a Shetland pony, children will have a brilliant time at a children's open farm. Wrap up warm and wash your hands before eating.

3. Find a pier

There are over 50 piers in the UK offering everything from fishing to entertainment. It's not all just amusement arcades and sweet shops. Punch and Judy and crab fishing are two enduring pier attractions that seem to have stood the test of time.

4. Village fair

Many country fairs have now veered away from the coconut shy and waltzers and go for organic grub and mums and dads races. Whatever your taste, Saturdays in May and June are always good for these.

5. Follow an abandoned railway line

They are now havens for wildlife and perfect for country walks.

6. Go on a nature trail

Look at leaves, insects, plants – anything you like in fact – and take a jam jar or two with you to bring back interesting finds.

7. Visit an activity centre

From whizzing down an aerial runway to wobbling on a crate stack, no previous experience is necessary at any one of the Scout Activity Centres. Find out how your child can attend as a Scout, with a school or youth group at www.scouts.org.uk/sac

8. Follow a coastal trail

From the magical North Norfolk Coastal path to bleakly beautiful beaches of Northumberland, why not get a little sand in your hiking boots this year.

9. Go folly hunting

The countryside is dotted with all manner of curious buildings, not all of which have a useful purpose. Find out about the follies in your local area at www.follies.org.uk.

10. Walk to a stately home

Even if you're not a member of the National Trust or English Heritage there are still many stately homes and gardens across the UK where you can wander through a piece of history.

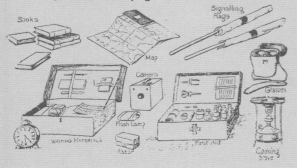

outdoor activities

10 UNUSUAL OUTDOOR ACTIVITIES

1. 3G swing

Two people sit in the seat and are slowly raised into the air. When they agree, the ripcord is pulled and they swing towards the ground at high speed – entirely safely!

2. Zorbing

Bouncing around inside a gigantic PVC ball, surrounded by a thick cushion of air. The inner and outer balls are held together by hundreds of nylon threads and then you are pushed down a hill, across a stretch of water or over the snow.

3. Grass sledging

Once a winter sport, sledging has been given the all-year round treatment with the start of grass sledging. Keep your arms and legs in the sled as you zoom down a hill.

4. Crate stacking

Not only do you have to work together, but you need to think together too, in order to build the tallest tower out of crates. This is the perfect activity for team-building as a person must be standing at the top of the crate tower at all times.

5. Aeroball

Combining volleyball, basketball and trampolining, this activity is guaranteed to leave your heart pounding as you compete for points against your opponents.

6. Land yachting

A land yacht is a wind propelled craft which looks like a long, thin, three-wheeled buggy with enough room for one person to sit inside and a sail attached to make it move. It normally takes place on large open areas of land where there is a minimum number of obstructions and as far away from other site users as possible. There are specialist clubs based across the UK providing training and taster days.

7. Coasteering

This activity will take you scrambling over rocks, jumping from cliffs, swimming in the sea, and getting washed by waves. You'll be scared and excited all at once.

8. Bungee running

Running as fast as you can towards a target is challenging enough, but is all the more fun when you are attached to a secured bungee cord. Are you strong enough to make it, or will you spring back to the start?

9. Pulling

Pulling involves travelling in a specialised pulling boat powered through the use of oars. It can be done as an individual or with up to eight people in a boat, promoting team work, cooperation and coordination. www.ara-rowing.org

10. Multi-pitch climbing

Ascending a rock feature, natural or manmade, can be exhilarating, but imagine trying a route that cannot be completed on one rope length. If this appeals, then multi-pitch climbing is for you!

GO GREEN

Grow your own picnic

If you have a garden, cultivate your own vegetable patch. You could start simple with herbs and salad items, or get advanced with runner beans and courgettes! Once the hard work is done, watch your picnic grow. Then go to a park or local beauty spot and enjoy eating it.

Take to the streets

Why not have a family challenge to see who can walk the furthest during the summer. You can buy simple pedometers very cheaply. Then put them in your pocket and they will calculate your footsteps. Remember to make a note of how far you have walked each day, and then record your results in the kitchen to see who goes the furthest. Walking is not just better for the environment, it's great for your health too.

Try a new outdoor adventure

With longer days and milder nights, summer is the ideal time to try something new outdoors. There's heaps of choice: horse riding, geocaching (treasure hunt game using GPS-enabled devices), field archery and coasteering are just a sample of what's out there.

Be a local tourist

There's no need to go miles to be a tourist (or get a tan!). Use the school holidays to explore some of the attractions closer to home. You could:

Enjoy a local nature walk

Visit a place of worship

Play games at your local park

Leave the car at home.

DON'T FORGET

• A camera: great for happy family shots, and even better for young people to build up a collection of pictures showing the weird and wonderful from woodland treks.

• Binoculars to get up close and personal with feathered, furry or finned creatures.

• Pens/pencils and a plain paper exercise book. You can use these to document flora and fauna on a nature trail, record old buildings on a local area history challenge or for writing the script for a short outdoor play. Involve friends and neighbours, and then invite parents to the finished performance.

• For every weather phenomenon the UK has to throw at you, sunscreen, hat(s), waterproofs and welly boots.

BEST EVER CAMPFIRE SONGS

My Bonnie Lies Over the Ocean

My bonnie lies over the ocean
My bonnie lies over the sea
My bonnie lies over the ocean
Oh bring back my bonnie to me
Bring back, bring back
Bring back my Bonnie to me, to me
Bring back, bring back
Bring back my Bonnie to me

The Animal Fair

We went to the animal fair, the birds and the
beasts were there,
The big baboon by the light of the moon was
combing his auburn hair.
The monkey slid out of his bunk, and slid down
the elephant's trunk,
The elephant sneezed and fell on his knees,
And that was the end of the monkey! (monkey,
monkey, monkey . . . etc.)

Campfire's Burning

Campfire's burning, campfire's burning
Draw nearer, draw nearer
In the gloaming, in the gloaming
Come sing and be merry (or Mary if you like)

Quartermaster's Store

There were rats, rats, as big as alley cats,
In the store, in the store.
There were rats, rats, as big as alley cats,
In the Quartermaster's store.

Chorus

My eyes are dim, I cannot see.
I have not brought my specs with me.

Repeat.
Mice . . . running through the rice.
Snakes . . . as big as garden rakes.
Beans . . . as big as submarines.
Gravy . . . enough to float the navy.
Cakes . . . that give us tummy aches.
Eggs . . . with scaly chicken legs.
Butter . . . running in the gutter.
Lard . . . they sell it by the yard.
Bread . . . with great big lumps like lead.
Cheese . . . that makes you want to sneeze.
Soot . . . they grow it by the foot.
Goats . . . eating all the oats.
Bees . . . with little knobbly knees.
Owls . . . shredding paper towels.
Apes . . . eating all the grapes.
Turtles . . . wearing rubber girdles.
Bear . . . with curlers in its hair.
Buffaloes . . . with hair between their toes.
Foxes . . . stuffed in little boxes.
Roaches . . . sleeping in the coaches.
Flies . . . swarming 'round the pies.
Fishes . . . washing all the dishes.
Moths . . . eating through the cloths.
Scouts . . . eating Brussels sprouts.

Oh You'll Never Get to Heaven

Oh you'll never get to heaven, in a rocking chair
'Cause the Lord don't allow, no lazybones there.

Chorus
I ain't gonna grieve my Lord.
I ain't gonna grieve my Lord.
I ain't gonna grieve my Lord no more.
I ain't gonna grieve, I 'aint gonna worry
I ain't gonna leave this world in a hurry
I ain't gonna grieve my Lord no more
Any more.

Oh you'll never get to heaven, in [name of person]'s car
'Cause the gosh darn thing, won't go that far…
Oh you'll never get to heaven, in [name of person]'s boat,
'Cause the gosh darn thing, won't even float…
Oh you'll never get to heaven, on water skis,
'Cause the Lord don't allow, no hairy knees…
Oh you'll never get to heaven, on roller skates,
'Cause you'll roll right by those pearly gates…
Oh you'll never get to heaven in a limousine,
'Cause the Lord don't sell no gasoline…

Oh you'll never get to heaven on a motor bike,
'Cause you'll get halfway, then you'll have to hike…
Oh you'll never get to heaven in a supersonic jet,
'Cause the Lord ain't got no runways yet…
Oh you'll never get to heaven with powder and paint,
'Cause it makes you look like what you ain't…
Oh you'll never get to heaven in a strapless gown,
'Cause the gosh darn thing might fall right down…
Oh you'll never get to heaven in [name of person]'s pants,
'Cause [name of person]'s pants are full of ants…
Oh I want to go to heaven, and I want to do it right,
So I'll go up to heaven all dressed in white…
Oh one fine day, and it won't be long,
You'll look for me, and I'll be gone…
Oh if you get to heaven, before I do,
Just bore a hole, and pull me through.
Well if I get to heaven, before you do.
I'll plug that hole, with shavings and glue…
That's all there is, there ain't no more.
Saint Peter said, as he closed the door…
Oh there's one more thing I forgot to tell,
If you don't go to heaven, you'll go to hell…

The Court of King Caractacus

Now, the ladies of the harem of the court of King Caractacus
were just passing by, (repeated 4 times)

Now, the noses on the faces of the ladies of the harem

Now, the boys who put the powder on the noses of the faces of the ladies

Now, the fascinating witches who put the scintillating stitches in the
britches of the boys who put the powder on the noses of the faces of the
ladies of the harem of the court of King Caractacus were just passing by

Now, the fascinating witches who put the scintillating stitches in the
britches of the boys who put the powder on the noses of the faces of the
ladies of the harem of the court of King Caractacus were just passing by

Now, if you want to take some pictures of the facinating witches who put
the scintillating stitches in the britches of the boy who put the powder
on the noses of the faces of the ladies of the harem of the court of

King Caractacus. . . you're too late. . .

Because they. . . just. . . passed. . . by.

Worms

Nobody likes me, everybody hates me,
I'll go out and dig some worms;
Long thin skinny ones;
Big fat juicy ones,
See how they wriggle and squirm.
Bite their heads off,
Suck their juice out,
Throw their skins away,
Nobody knows how much I thrive
On worms three times a day.
Long thin skinny ones slip down easily,
Big fat juicy ones stick;
Hold your head back,
Squeeze their tail,
And their juice just goes drip, drip.

10 in the Bed

There were 10 in the bed, and the little one
said, roll over, roll over,
So they all rolled over and one fell out, and
banged his head and began to shout,
Please remember, to tie a knot in my
pyjamas.
Single beds are only made for...

1, 2, 3, 4, 5, 6, 7, 8, 9
*Repeat over and over, dropping one number each time
around until there's no one left in bed.*

There's a Hole in My Bucket

H = Henry
L = Liza

H There's a hole in my bucket, dear Liza, dear Liza
There's a hole in my bucket, dear Liza, a hole.

L Then fix it, dear Henry, dear Henry, dear Henry
Then fix it, dear Henry, dear Henry, dear Henry.

H With what shall I fix it?
L With straw.
H The straw is too long.
L Then cut it.
H With what shall I cut it?
L With an axe.
H The axe is too dull.
L Then sharpen it.
H With what shall I sharpen it?
L With a stone.
H But the stone is too dry.
L Then wet it.
H With what shall I wet it?
L With water.
H With what shall I fetch it?
L With a bucket.
H But there's a hole in my bucket!

Do Your Ears Hang Low?

[Tune: Turkey in the Straw, refrain]
Do your ears hang low, do they waggle to and fro?
Can you tie them in a knot, can you tie them in a bow?
Can you throw them o'er your shoulder like a regimental soldier?
Do your ears hang low?

Do your ears stick out, can you waggle them about?
Can you flap them up and down as you fly around the town?
Can you shut them up for sure when you hear an awful bore?
Do your ears stick out?

Do your ears stand high, do they reach up to the sky?
Do they hang down when they're wet, do they stand up when they're dry?
Can you semaphore your neighbour with the minimum of labour?
Do your ears stand high?

Goin' on a Bear Hunt

Goin' on a bear hunt.
Goin' to catch a big one.
I'm not afraid.
Look, what's up ahead?
Mud!
Can't go over it.
Can't go under it.
Can't go around it.
Gotta go through it. *Make sloshing sounds and move hands as if slogging.*
Sticks. *Snap fingers.*
Tree. *Make gestures climbing up and down.*
Gate. *Make gate-opening gestures.*
River. *Make swimming gestures.*
Cave. *Go in it and find bear. Reverse all motions quicky to get home.*

INDEX

About Nick Allen

A professional chef who has been involved in Scouting from the age of six, this is Nick Allen's first book. After studying for an NVQ in professional cookery, Nick was appointed as a commis chef at the world-famous Dorchester Hotel in Mayfair. Over the course of five years he worked his way up to the position of Senior chef de partie. He is now sous chef at the Dorchester Collection's Coworth Park Hotel, a country manor in Ascot with three restaurants.

When he's not running the kitchen of Michelin-starred executive chef Chris Meredith, Nick is often to be found cooking eggs in oranges over an open fire at scout camp. An assistant explorer scout leader with the 1st explorer scout unit in Tonbridge, Kent, he has travelled the world on Scouting expeditions and cooked at many a Jamboree.

About Bear Grylls

Bear Grylls is the UK's youngest chief scout, appointed in May 2009. Whether it is crossing the Atlantic Arctic Ocean in an open boat, scaling Mount Everest or flying a powered paraglider to 29,000ft in the Himalayas, Bear knows a thing or two about adventure. But he is not just about breaking records in the great outdoors.

As an ex Special Forces soldier, he is not only known around the world as the host of the hit TV series *Born Survivor* and *Man vs Wild*, he is also an inspirational speaker, bestselling author and a fervent supporter of young people getting out there to experience adventure for themselves.

Bear got his taste for the outdoors as a cub scout, whilst a young boy. He was taught to climb by his father on the sea cliffs of the Isle of Wight, and this interest rapidly developed when he left school.

His military service saw him trained in combat survival, parachuting, demolitions, trauma medics and mountain warfare as a trooper

with 21 SAS. During one parachute jump he sustained a massive injury, breaking his back in three places. After intense military rehabilitation, he made a full recovery and went on to become one of the youngest climbers ever to reach the summit of Everest and has led numerous other expeditions around the world. He has since been awarded an honorary commission in the Royal Navy as a Lieutenant-Commander, in recognition of his adventurous feats and his determination to help charities and young people.

When invited to take on this role with UK's largest co-educational youth movement, Bear said, 'I feel so honoured to be offered this position, and have always held such admiration for scouts and all they do around the world. The Scouting movement is a massive force for good, touching many, many young lives.'

About The Scout Association

The Scout Association offers fun, challenge and everyday adventure to 400,000 boys and girls across the UK. It is a charity incorporated by Royal Charter making a positive impact on young people, adult volunteers and local communities. For flexible volunteering opportunities visit www.scouts.org.uk.

Acknowledgements

Thank you to everyone who has contributed in any way to this book, especially our Scouting supporters and chief scout, Bear Grylls.

Thanks also to The Scout Holiday Homes Trust, Claire Woodforde, Beth Gooch, Hermione Clulow, Nicola Gordon-Wilson, Richard Chambers, Hilary Galloway, Sam Avery and Chris James at The Scout Association and Stuart Cooper and Claire Potter at Metrostar Media.

A final thank you to all volunteers for Scouting who provide activities and opportunities for young people in the UK and around the world.